EUROPE UNDER THE OLD REGIME

EUROPE UNDER THE OLD REGIME

BY

ALBERT SOREL

TRANSLATED BY

FRANCIS H. HERRICK

HARPER TORCHBOOKS
THE ACADEMY LIBRARY

HARPER & ROW, PUBLISHERS
New York

EUROPE UNDER THE OLD REGIME

Copyright, 1947, by Francis H. Herrick

Printed in the United States of America.

This book was translated from the French by Francis H. Herrick and originally published in 1947 by The Ward Ritchie Press, Los Angeles, California.

First HARPER TORCHBOOK edition published 1964 by
Harper & Row, Publishers, Incorporated
49 East 33rd Street
New York 16, N.Y.

INTRODUCTION

ALBERT SOREL stands among the first historians of Europe because of his elaborate study entitled *L'Europe et la révolution française*, which appeared in eight volumes between 1885 and 1904. His whole life was devoted either to preparation for or to the completion of this great work. Sorel was born in Normandy in 1842 and trained in the law. In 1866 he entered the foreign office under Napoleon III, and gained valuable practical experience of diplomacy during the period of the fall of the second empire and the establishment of the third republic. In 1872 he was appointed to the chair of diplomatic history at the *École libre des sciences politiques* in Paris, and in 1875 he left the foreign office to become the secretary general of the *Présidence du sénat*. There his light official duties permitted him leisure for the scrupulous historical researches upon which his literary work was founded. *L'Europe et la révolution francaise* was recognized as a classic when the first volume appeared in 1885. It received the Gobert grand prize and was crowned by the French Academy, and the work was crowned a second time when the second volume came out in 1887. The author died in 1906, only two years after the final volume was published and in the same year that the completed history was awarded the Osiris prize by the Institute of France.

Sorel's work clearly represents not only an improvement on von Sybel's *Geschichte der Revolutionszeit von 1789-1800*, but also a reaction against the point of view of Taine, whose theories of scientific social and intellectual history had paradoxically resulted in his brilliantly prejudiced studies of the old regime and the French revolution. The doctrinaire theories of the revolutionaries, to Sorel, were neither to be attacked nor supported; they were merely a cloak under which the living body of national interest remained unchanged. He was not interested in theories of society, but in the attitude of individual men towards their interests and their times, and the way in which many such views combined to create the substance and the continuity of diplomacy. When viewed in this light, Sorel's masterpiece becomes much more than a conventional diplomatic history, that is, a mine of information based upon painstaking research and meant only for scholars; it is a complete account of the way in which the lasting realities of European history came to a climax in an age of revolution and conquest.

The initial chapter, which is here translated into English for the first time, provides the background for the whole eight-volume history. Although over half a century old, it is still the best analysis of the European state system in the eighteenth century and the classic introduction to the study of revolutionary and Napoleonic diplomacy. Even more striking, however, is its contemporary interest. Though recent monographs may have corrected particular points in other sections, time has not affected the significance of Sorel's general views. His introductory survey illuminates the revolutions and conquests of the twentieth century as clearly as those of Robespierre and Bonaparte.

This translation adheres closely to the original, although footnotes have been omitted since scholars interested in them will prefer to use the complete French text. Two footnotes which seemed essential have been incorporated in the body of the translation and Montesquieu's reference to preventive wars has been supplied. The English of the passage on conquests by Rabelais, in Section VI, is that of Sir Thomas Urquhart's seventeenth-century translation. Occasionally the paragraph structure has been altered and a few explanatory phrases have been added, but such changes have been made only when required for clarity. Mr. Edmund Masson, formerly of the Department of French at Mills College and now at the University of California, was of great assistance in preparing the translation. I wish to record both recognition of his scholarship and gratitude for his aid, although responsibility for the present form is my own. Finally, I am indebted to my wife in many ways, and in particular for preparing the index.

Mills College   Francis H. Herrick

EUROPE UNDER THE OLD REGIME

ON BEGINNING THIS HISTORY, the reader must disabuse himself of one conception. It is that of regarding the Europe of the old regime as a society of states, regularly constituted, in which each conformed its conduct to principles generally recognized by all, in which respect for established law governed negotiations and dictated treaties, in which good faith directed the execution of them, and in which the feeling of solidarity among monarchies assured the permanence of engagements contracted by princes, together with the maintenance of public order. After the beginning of modern times, this "Christian Republic," as some have been pleased to call it, was never more than an august abstraction. It had seemingly been realized for a brief moment in the middle ages; but the uncertain outlines disappeared when the great dream of the papacy—the government of the Catholic world by a theocracy—vanished into thin air. The Renaissance ruined this conception, just as it had ruined the feudal system and scholastic philosophy. Nothing remained but vague memories with which Utopians rocked themselves to sleep.

A Europe in which the rights of everyone resulted from duties for all was something so strange to the statesmen of the old regime that the Revolutionary and the Napoleonic Wars, lasting a quarter of a century and the most formidable yet seen, were required to impose the idea upon them and demonstrate its necessity. The attempt to give Europe an elementary organization at the Congress of Vienna and in the Congresses which followed was a step forward, not a return to the past. In the eighteenth century such progress was only one of the beautiful theories of philosophers. As the year 1789 approached, it began to insinuate itself into the minds of various political leaders, particularly in France, but they were considered dreamers. The great majority of the rulers of Europe, confounding this design with the chimera of perpetual peace, continued to consider it as the ultimate in paradoxes.

Nevertheless, though no Christian republic existed in Europe, there were nations and states. Ever since nations and states have existed and have had relations with each other, there has been a law of nations. As Montesquieu said, "all peoples recognize a law of nations, even the Iroquois." The Europe of the old regime observed certain practices, to which attention should be paid, rather than to the international law which reformers proposed as an ideal for future society. Voltaire said of such proposals, "They seem a consolation to peoples for the wrongs done them by politics and force." The acts of governments had reality; the problem of the historian is to understand the established practices by which their relationships were regulated. These practices were never regarded as laws derived from a few abstract principles, but rather as the simple definition of relationships based on the very nature of things. "International law is founded upon facts," wrote Bielfeld, a writer justly considered as an authority by diplomats. "To understand it, one must know history, which is the soul of this science, as it is of politics in general."

IN SUCH AN INTERNATIONAL LAW, the one fundamental conception was that of the state. It dominated and ruled all political life. It was the state in the spirit of Rome, a collective being, a sovereign and absolute master. In Rome it had been incarnated in the person of a prince to whom was attributed "majesty," or the omnipotent authority which pertained to the Republic. The Christian idea of a prince chosen by God as the representative of divinity on earth and the feudal idea of the monarch as universal overlord were both added to this conception. In this way the concept of the sovereign was formed, a concept understood by the whole continent in the terms used by Bossuet: "All the state is concentrated in the person of the prince. In him is the power, in him is the will of the whole people." He was clothed with this majesty because the monarch was the state itself; he held it of the state, and the state possessed this majesty even if there were no monarch to personify it. It is significant that the principle of divine right, by which individual sovereigns were considered as holding their rights from divinity itself, was applied to the state before it was applied to persons, and was but one consequence of the doctrine that all power comes from God. Such a doctrine made no distinction between either the form or the mode of transmission of power. In the words of Bossuet, "The people must remain in the condition to which they have been accustomed by the passage of time; this is why God takes under his protection all legitimate governments, in whatever form they may be." "By Him all kings reign, both those whom birth establishes and those who come by election, because He presides at all councils. There is no power on earth which He has not ordained. *No authority exists unless it comes from God*, says the oracle of the Scripture."

The pope, the emperor of Germany, and the king of Poland were elected, but no distinctions were drawn between their rights and those of the king of France. When Napoleon, placing on his head the crown of Italy, pronounced the sacramental formula: "God has given it to me, let those who would harm it beware!" he was not twisting the meaning nor did he risk scandalizing the old Europe; he was merely speaking its language. "Charlemagne," say the *Memoirs of Louis XIV*, "mounted to the pinnacle of glory, not by the favor of some prince but by courage and victories, which are the election and suffrages of heaven itself when it has resolved to place other powers under one sole ruler."

For this reason it was necessary to veil the origin of authority. In such a system of law, prescription was everything, and there was nothing of which the foundations were more obscure. The mystery by which fact legitimized itself was conveniently kept out of sight in formidable shadows, hazardous to explore. Above all, it was important that the people should not force an entry into the sanctuary. "It must never come to pass," said Pascal, "that we sense the fact of usurpation; authority was introduced in other times without reason and has become reasonable; we must make it seem authentic, eternal, and conceal the beginning if we do not not wish it to come to an end." On this subject the practical man agreed with the philosopher. "The rights of peoples and the prerogatives of kings never agree so well as in silence," wrote the Cardinal de Retz. The skepticism of the eighteenth century led to the same conclusion. Voltaire could declare, without provoking the censure of chancelleries and without drawing upon himself the blame of European courts, "Time, occasion, usage, prescription, force, these are the only laws." Such were the fundamental thoughts of the men who were conducting the affairs of Europe towards the close of the eighteenth century. —

Sovereignty in other states became legitimate only by the recognition which was granted. Recognition, however, did not imply any reflection on the origin of power in the new state. It was even admitted that relationships between states existed which were independent of the form of government or of revolutions which might modify it. In the words of M. de Bordeaux, sent over to England by Louis XIV and admitted before the parliament of the Commonwealth on December 21, 1652: "The connections which should exist between neighboring states are not determined by the form of governments; for this reason, even though it has pleased God in his providence to change the government formerly established in this country, there is still the necessity of commerce and communication between France and England; this kingdom has been able to change its form and from a monarchy become a Commonwealth; but the geographical situation does not change at all, the two peoples remain neighbors interested in each other because of commerce, and the treaties which exist between the two nations concern the peoples more than the princes since their principal object is common utility."

All types of government existed in Europe, and all were considered equally legitimate. A theocracy existed in the Papal States, autocracy in Russia, pure despotism at Constantinople, absolute monarchy in France, Spain, the states of the Austrian Royal house, and Prussia. There was a constitutional monarchy in England, an empire formed out of a confederation of states in Germany, federal republics in the United Provinces of the Netherlands and in Switzerland, and a republic with an elected king in Poland. Finally, in Venice, Genoa, Ragusa and the Free Cities of Germany were found all the varieties of republican government which had come down from the middle ages. "To preserve our social order we have developed three kinds of states: royal, seigneurial, and popular," wrote Pasquier, a jurist of the sixteenth century. "Each legislator considers his own the best."

In the eighteenth century the forms were called monarchy, aristocracy, and democracy. They were studied in relation to their purpose, which was the good of the state; but no one dreamed of establishing any sort of hierarchy among them. Men of the world had thought for a long time that the most reasonable and expedient plan was "to esteem the state where one was born the best of all, and to submit to it." Such was the doctrine of the Church.

Even Montesquieu, the man who had studied most profoundly and explained best the constitutions of states, followed this prudent rule: "I am a good citizen, but I would have been one in no matter what country I might have been born. I am a good citizen because I love the government under which I was born."

The idea of attributing to some one constitution an absolute superiority over others, the idea that there might exist an ideal constitution applicable to all countries, or above all the idea of making it an object of propaganda never entered the minds of statesmen. The words "republic" and "democracy" were never associated with the idea of revolution. Republican and democratic forms were thought of as suited only to small states; they went along with peaceful habits and a modest policy. The Commonwealth of England was considered an exception; but it would not have been strong except for Cromwell. The other republics attracting attention were more or less declining; some seemed to be menaced, none were menacing. The Swiss cantons inclined towards neutrality; the United Provinces of the Netherlands were absorbed in business; Venice was subsiding solemnly; Poland was dissolving into anarchy. "Sweden," wrote Frederick the Great, "experienced the fate of every monarchical state which changes itself into a republic: she grew feeble." When a great republic was formed in North America towards the end of the century, the monarchies of the continent considered it from this point of view. "It takes time to form a conquering people," was the word passed in the chancelleries. "In a republic it is even more difficult to instil the spirit of conquest than in a government embodied in one man." The statesmen of the old Europe judged the French revolution at its beginning from the same point of view. They looked on it as a weakening of the French state, and their conduct consequently depended upon whether this seemed prejudicial or advantageous to their policy.

III

THE STATE EMBODIED its own ends. It was sovereign; it recognized no authority above its own. "They are Gods," ran the doctrine. "No one but God may judge their judgments or their persons." Even catholic sovereigns did not concede superiority to the Pope. Outside of questions of dogma, he was a prince like the others. "Who can be judge of such things?" wrote Richelieu. "Who can consider them without passion and without prejudice? Certainly not the Pope, who is a temporal prince and has not renounced the grandeurs of the earth so completely as to be indifferent to them. God alone can be the judge. Therefore, kings cannot sin but against Him, to whom alone belongs the cognizance of their actions." Appealing to God in these terms was appealing to history, which alone can reveal the designs of Providence. In reality, some direction and some standard of judgment was necessary in the system of related facts and in the stream of life. The state could find them nowhere but in itself. It drew them out of its own omnipotence. The final cause in all things was the "reason of state," which meant the old doctrine of public safety, such as Rome had practiced and had taught to the world. It had never disappeared from political life. The Renaissance returned the "reason of state" to a place of honor, and its development paralleled the formation of the great modern states. They borrowed from Rome the spirit for their polity as well as the model for their institutions.

The name of Machiavelli is rightly linked with this doctrine; but Machiavelli was less a theorizer than an observer, all the force of his work coming from the character of reality with which he invested it. He described what he saw and merely used the statecraft of his contemporaries as his guiding principle. So thought Richelieu, who considered the doctrines of "this solid and inspired writer" to be "indispensable," and never failed to find inspiration in them. One reads in an *Apology for Machiavelli* composed by a disciple of the cardinal: "His doctrines are as old as time and as states. He teaches nothing that is particular in application or out of the ordinary, but recounts only what our predecessors have done and what men of today practice usefully, innocently, and inevitably."

The most profound thinker and the greatest statesman of old France, Pascal and Richelieu, were agreed on this point, and the agreement was not a matter of chance. The former said, "States would perish if laws were not frequently bent before necessity. . . . Not being able to strengthen justice, men justify strength." The latter, who applied the doctrine of public safety with so much rigor, pushed it to its final consequences in his *Political Testament*. "In matters of state, he who has the power often has the right, and he who is weak can only with difficulty keep from being wrong in the opinion of the majority of the world." The reign of Louis XIV did not change the general opinion. "The supreme law which is the reason of state," in the words of Saint-Simon, continued to govern princes. In the eighteenth century but one exception can be found, and it is of the sort which confirms the rule: namely, Frederick the Great and his *Anti-Machiavel*. When Frederick composed this dissertation, his ambitions were confined to school. As soon as he was free from leading strings, he threw his schoolboy notebooks to the four winds of Europe and intrigued for things quite different from the prizes of virtue. Machiavelli had his revenge in the career of Frederick. The Revolutionary period at the end of the century held even more spectacular revenges for him, but this was not unexpected nor was it surprising to well-informed minds. "Everyone decries this author," said a friend of Mazarin, "but everyone follows him in practice, and principally those who decry him." In the eighteenth century, both thought and character were on a lower plane. Instead of the lofty irony of a Pascal and the rough sincerity of a Richelieu, the disparaging raillery of Voltaire and the cynicism of Frederick the Great set the fashion. In general the parallel can be continued. Thought became more complaisant towards actions more licentious. But, though refining itself in this way, perverting itself further, and complicating itself with a more subtle depravity, the reason of state reigned more despotically than ever.

It reigned wherever men felt strong enough to follow with impunity the designs it suggested. It inspired the same talk at Vienna and at Berlin. It was taught to young princes and to future ministers. The *Political Institutions* of Bielfeld stated: "In whatever situation a state may find itself, the fundamental principle of the reason of state is ever the same. This principle, adopted by all ancient and modern peoples, is that the safety of the people should ever be the supreme law." "The great powers," wrote an Austrian diplomat in 1791, "must act in conformity with the reason of state. . . . Interest must overcome every sort of resentment, no matter how right it may be."

The reason of state being the rule, aggrandizement became the object of statecraft. "He who gains nothing, loses," wrote Catherine II. The concept of the grandeur of the state was intimately linked with that of the extent of the state. Such ideas are as old as human society. As soon as men were grouped together, they fought to conquer and to defend themselves. Spoliation and conquest are as ancient as covetousness, and envy was born with mankind. In all ages princes have done honor to this point of view. "It is," said Machiavelli, "a very natural and ordinary thing to desire to extend and amplify one's boundaries, and when men are able to do so and make the attempt, they are highly praised, or at least not reprehended." Machon, the apologist of the seventeenth century, developed this rule. It is founded, he said, "on these principles and truths—that among princes, who have nothing but what they have usurped, the strongest make the law for the weaker and take what is for their own good because they believe whatever is convenient is right, and that states have no other end than their own preservation even to the prejudice of that of their neighbors." In the following century, such ideas led Montesquieu to conclude: "War and expansion are the essence of monarchy."

IV

WITH THE PRINCIPLES AND OBJECTS of statesmanship set forth in this way, the rules of conduct can be deduced. The most important was that one must always be on the trail of opportunities in order to seize them. "He who negotiates always finds at last the proper moment for attaining his end." Success was to the foresighted and the clever. The chances had to be reckoned, without a doubt, but the chances profited the superior men, for failure was usually the work of blunderers. In the words of Bossuet, "Though in particular instances fortune seems to decide the creation or the ruin of empires, in the long run things turn out much as a game of chance, where the most skillful win in the end. Indeed, in the bloody game in which peoples have struggled for empire and for power, the nation which has looked ahead the farthest, has applied itself the most, has persevered longest in its great labors, and, finally, has known best whether to advance or retreat according to the situation, has in the end secured the advantage, and made fortune the servant of its designs."

The majesty of such words must not blind us to the character of the facts. Never did more ample euphemisms disguise the misdeeds of less scrupulous policies. We must leave the galleries where Bossuet painted such vast word frescoes; we must enter the cabinet of the statesman, despoiling him of his courtly costume and processional posture, and show him as he is. La Bruyère gives a finished portrait of him; whoever appreciates it has nothing more to learn of the statecraft of the time.

"The minister and plenipotentiary is a chameleon, a Proteus"; but he only changes his expression knowingly and for a good reason. "He considers the time, the place, the occasion, his strength or his weakness, the genius of the nations with which he treats, the temperament and character of the persons with whom he

· 12 ·

negotiates. All his views, all his statements, all the refinements of his policy tend to one sole end—which is never to be deceived himself and always to deceive others." One of the surest means of achieving his end is even to speak the truth; this is an art in which he excels. "He is ponderous and dissimulating to hide a fact while stating it, because it must be said yet must not be believed, or else he is frank and open so that, when he conceals what must not be known, it will be supposed that he has omitted nothing which anyone might wish to know, and that he has said all." He supports his allies, "if he finds it useful and likely to advance his policy"; he even supports the weak against the strong "in order to keep the balance even," only he sells dearly his protection and alliance and then supports the strong to upset the balance again. In addition, he is a man of the world, a gentleman above all things, exquisite in his manners. He understands all the nuances of speech, he is a master of those suited to each occasion, he excels in finding noble pretexts. "He speaks only of peace, of alliances, of public tranquillity, of public welfare; while in fact he thinks only of his own interests, which are those of his master or his government." But he is not the dupe of his own phrases, and never ends by believing them. "Above all, he strives to secure the solid and essential things with his intrigues, and is always ready to sacrifice details and points of imaginary honor."

In the eighteenth century forms were altered, but only the forms. The fashionable phrases and the accepted pretexts changed with the taste of the day and the reigning doctrine. Persiflage was in vogue, and skepticism lent authority. The statesman affected disbelief even in his own ability. "Everyone," according to Voltaire, "has received from nature the desire to better his position. An opportunity appears; an intriguer seizes it; a woman, gained by money or by her feelings, opposes the negotiation; another supports it. Circumstances, fancy, caprice, suspicion—some trifle decides the issue." "So the world goes," concluded Frederick the Great. "It is ruled by favoritism and gossip." At bottom Frederick did not believe this, and, though sacrificing in public to what he called "the good goddess, Her Sacred Majesty

Chance," he was ever the most deliberate, the most sagacious, and the least reckless of statesmen. He had his table talk—and his private philosophy. The latter was like that of Richelieu. "Let us not deceive ourselves; fortune and chance are words with no real significance.—Seize the favorable opportunity for an undertaking, but never force the occasion and abandon everything to chance.—Political life demands patience; the supreme achievement of the clever man is the performance of each act in its proper time.—He whose conduct is best calculated, triumphs over those who act with less consistency." Such were the innermost thoughts which never changed.

When the wind turned to philosophy, the statesman became a philosopher. He loved the truth, he was humanitarian, he called himself "citizen"; he preached tolerance; he spoke only of the happiness of the human race; good manners and the art of living led him to become *virtuous* instead of *genteel*, as he had been in the preceding century. Of course it was an easy virtue, of the same nature as the gentility which it replaced. There was nothing modest about it, nothing which implied abstaining from anything. It was enough to be a gallant man, free from prejudices, careful of conventions, proper in speech, and observant of the fine distinctions in life. But for the scandal regarding Baron von Trenck, whom he imprisoned for eighteen years, Frederick would have passed as a "humanitarian." If he had left the church with less notoriety, Talleyrand would have had "virtue." The statesman showed sensibility when necessary; he grew enthusiastic, he loved nature, he shed tears. Diplomacy, which had its rationalists, would have its sentimentalists as well. "She weeps, and always takes!" said Frederick of Maria Theresa after the partition of Poland.

In reality, therefore, the world went on in the same way, and all these refinements led but to the same end, "which was never to be deceived, and always to deceive the others." This was understood, and relationships were marked by an incurable suspicion which was but too well founded. "A State," wrote a former minister of foreign affairs, "must always be on guard, like a worldly man who lives among violent and quarrelsome people. Since such are the nations of Europe, today, more than ever, negotiations are but a continual quarrel between people without conscience, bold in acquisition, and ever unsatisfied."

V

The reason of state directed all policy, and state interest was the only guarantee of any engagements. In other words, no guarantee existed at all. There never had been much at any time. In the sixteenth century, Bodin stated the fact sadly: "During the last two or three hundred years the opinion has taken root that no treaty is too solemn to be violated. As a result the opinion has almost acquired the force of a rule that a prince, forced to make a disadvantageous peace or treaty, may disregard it whenever the opportunity arises." The seventeenth century went farther than the sixteenth in this respect, and the eighteenth surpassed them both. At the beginning of his *Memoirs*, Frederick the Great treated of "reasons for breaking alliances." He distinguished four: the defection of the allied state, the necessity of forestalling such a defection, superior force, insufficiency of means. He forgot a fifth, which was the most frequent and which he knew from experience: the reason of state, or political interest, whichever it was called. Like Machiavelli, Frederick was only describing the manners of his time. When he made this statement, he was not writing a satire, but actually drawing up a protocol. "In dealing with madmen, knaves, personal enemies and competitors," said Cardinal Dubois, who was of the same stamp, "prudence demands that no engagements be made without great precautions."

No precautions were sufficient against unrestrained covetousness and the sophistries of the reason of state. This was made apparent, in the middle of the eighteenth century, by the war of the Austrian succession, which revealed manners as they really were. Charles VI had exhausted all the resources and guarantees of international law to assure his daughter, Maria Theresa, the succession to his hereditary estates. He established her rights by an organic law, the *Pragmatic Sanction*, and secured its confirmation from all the diets of the monarchy. He obtained solemn renunciations from pretenders. The *Pragmatic Sanction* was then communicated to all the powers, who recognized it expressly and engaged in formal treaties to respect it eternally. Nevertheless, on the very morrow of the death of Charles VI, the princes who had renounced their claims to his heritage and those who had guaranteed it to his daughter, tore up their signatures, violated their pledges, and leagued themselves to divide the spoils of Maria Theresa. Never before had the reason of state been opposed more impudently to the most elementary laws of honor and justice. England alone kept her engagements; but it should be observed that her interests and desires encouraged her to keep faith. Such were the customs of the time, and the customs of the whole of Europe. At the end of the century the Count de Segur, a French diplomat and a most gallant gentleman, both intelligent and reasonable, commented as follows on the work of a celebrated writer who was an implacable adversary of the house of Hapsburg: "What Favier says of the lack of respect for treaties and of the bad faith of the cabinet of Vienna is quite true, but unfortunately history proves that the same truth applies to all the cabinets of Europe."

The international law which the states practiced against each other grew out of this background. "In matters of politics," said Baron Bielfeld, "one must not be deceived by speculative ideas which the common people form of justice, equity, moderation, candor, and the other virtues of nations and their leaders. *In the end everything is reduced to force.*" In fact, force carried everything with it, even up to approbation, whch was secured in a measure along with all the worth-while things which were usurped. Cynics declared quite bluntly that the end justified the means; and wise men were forced to admit that if it did not justify them, it caused them to be forgotten. Vergennes, a statesman of the last years of the French monarchy, wrote that the supposition that the king of Prussia was making himself hated should not permit complaisance towards the success of his enterprises. "With the passage of time, hatred of the methods of expansion of a monarchy is dissipated, and the power remains." This attitude towards honor itself must be appreciated to grasp the spirit of the times. Montesquieu, treating of education in monarchies, wrote: "Here the actions of men are considered not as good, but beautiful; not as just but splendid; not as reasonable but extraordinary. When honor finds an element of nobility in any deeds it becomes either the judge who legitimizes or the sophist who justifies them. . . . It permits cunning when associated with the idea of greatness of soul or importance in affairs, as in political matters, the subtleties of which are not offensive to honor. It forbids adulation only when separated from the thought of great fortune."

War was the great instrument of rule, the supreme argument of the reason of state. It was considered right as soon as it was judged necessary. It was waged to conquer or to preserve, in self-defense against an attack or to forestall one. When Coligny was urging Charles IX to make a surprise attack on Spain, which was threatening France, he concluded that "It is better to set fire to the house of one's neighbor than to wait until he sets it to yours." Henry IV of France remarked, "Great kings must resolve to be hammers or anvils, and I would rather give two blows to my enemies than receive one from their hands." Descartes, who never took pride in Machiavellism, considered that such arguments were not unphilosophical. "In relations between sovereigns," he said to a great lady asking his opinion of the political theories in the *Prince*, "justice has different limits than for individuals. . . . One must also distinguish between subjects, friends or allies, and enemies; because, with respect to the latter, a prince has a quasi-permission to do anything, provided that some advantage is secured for him or his subjects. In this case I do not disapprove joining the fox with the lion and adding artifice to force. I even consider as enemies all who are neither friends nor allies, because one has the right to make war on such whenever it seems advantageous and because one has reason to mistrust them when they become suspect and powerful." The famous passage on preventive wars in *The Spirit of the Laws* is but a resume of these old commonplaces. According to Montesquieu: "With individuals the right of natural defence does not imply a necessity of attacking. . . . But with states the right of natural defence carries along with it sometimes the necessity of attacking—as, for instance, when one nation sees that a continuance of peace will enable another to destroy it, and that immediate attack is the only means of preventing its own destruction."

Since making war to forestall a danger was considered legitimate, attack without warning to surprise the enemy and to foil his plans was judged necessary. The brutal aggressions, the surprise attacks, and the robber conquests of Frederick the Great have often been cited. Yet he did nothing but undertake with audacity and execute with good fortune what his contemporaries meditated without daring or attempted without succeeding. "A great power with a great design," Louis XV's private advisor, the Count of Broglie, told him, "first carries it out in spite of general indignation. Then it makes the reckoning with its neighbors, and the balance of the account is always favorable."

In 1755 the English attacked the French on the sea, without warning and without a declaration of war. At the Court of Versailles it was supposed they were in accord with the Austrians. "The military leaders," reported Bernis, "were of the opinion that the English aggression should be regarded as the first step of a project meditated for a long time and agreed upon with the allies of England; and that, as a consequence, it was necessary to occupy the Austrian Netherlands to upset their plans." The king of Prussia urged them on with the assurance that he would invade Bohemia with 140,000 men while the French were securing Belgium. Fortunately he was not listened to, because he was negotiating a treaty with England directed against France at the same time that he was suggesting these captious proposals to France, his ally. These events occurred in the months of July and August, 1755. Maria Theresa was informed of them, and at the beginning of September she revealed the defection of Frederick to Louis XV, and proposed that he turn the tables and attack Prussia "to set just limits to her ambitions." Louis XV refused; he would hear only of a defensive alliance. Maria Theresa addressed herself to the Russians, and, on the 25th of March, 1756 her ambassador at Petersburg declared that she was ready to attack Frederick with 80,000 men. She hastened "to launch the affair," Bernis tells us, and she was right, for it was impossible to imagine Frederick waiting to attack his enemies until they had had the time to form their coalition. "Shall I let her tweak my nose?" he said to the English minister. "This woman wishes war and she shall have it. I can do nothing but get the start on my enemies. My troops are ready; the coalition must be broken before it becomes too strong." He invaded Saxony and marched on Bohemia. So began the Seven Years War.

These events were typical and set a precedent. In 1792 the French proponents of war with Austria did not fail to use the example of Frederick in 1756 to justify the attack which they advocated.

VI

STATES RECOGNIZED no other judges but themselves, and no other law but their own interests, yet the consequences of excess in this doctrine tempered it in practice. Common sense was the antidote to the paradoxes of the reason of state; interests well understood were a check to the allurements of covetousness. In reality, no other rules were known, and this was the sole foundation of international justice. Ambition dictated the plan; prudence governed the execution. Frederick held it necessary to know when to stop, because "To force happiness is to lose it, and always wishing for more is the way of never being content." This was a very practical moral, or rather it was not a moral at all, it was still calculation and politics.

Long ago it was said concerning Alexander the Great, that though petty thieves are punished with death, altars are erected to great ones. In the old regime, emphasis and proportion were everything. He who made himself illustrious by taking a province, was despised for seizing a village. Some petty skirmish in which a village was burned passed for a massacre; a battle in which thousands of men were slaughtered was a glorious action. The prejudices of the world had to be considered. Though it was sometimes necessary to fly in the face of them in great enterprises, it was always useless to arouse them by petty irritations. The venial sins were those which opinion pardoned the least in its heroes. For this reason, the consciences of statesmen appeared as scrupulous in small matters as they were complaisant to great injustices. "It is bad to break one's word without cause," said Frederick, "it gives one the reputation of being a changeable and flighty man." Richelieu thought that, everything considered, observing treaties was the wisest practice, saying "The greatest strength of sovereigns comes from doing this." For the same reason, usurpation demanded a good excuse. "As for the duchy of Warsaw," wrote the king of Prussia, "I abstained from taking it because the game was not worth the candle. The slice was so thin that it would not have made up for the opposition aroused. When a little thing is taken eagerly, it gives one the character of avarice and insatiability." Frederick came immediately to this cynical conclusion, and was proud of it. Examinations of her conscience led Maria Theresa through many tears to a similar capitulation. "One must resign oneself to taking a slim profit without losing one's reputation before God and before men," she wrote to her minister Kaunitz. The fact is that she resigned herself on a large scale. In 1772 the day came when the august matron of Vienna and the philosopher of Sans Souci met, shook hands, and received communion from the body of Poland. The empress took while weeping, and the king smiled cynically while taking, but the only difference between them was that the former claimed from the latter a bit more of Poland as a recompense for her remorse and an additional number of Poles to relieve her scruples. She received them, and this was the only satisfaction accorded to morality in the affair.

Conquest, which was the initial reason and the crowning achievement of all enterprises, was limited by its own purposes. The abuse of force destroyed its achievements. It was necessary to be strong to conquer, but it was necessary to be just and wise to keep. Rabelais, who had observed in the French monarchy the example of wisely conceived and skillfully carried out conquests, set forth the principle in magnificent words. "The manner of preserving and retaining countries newly conquered in obedience is not, as hath been the erroneous opinion of some tyrannical spirits to their own detriment and dishonor, to pillage, plunder, force, spoil, trouble, oppress, vex, disquiet, ruin and destroy the people, ruling, governing, and keeping them in awe with rods of iron. . . . Like babes new born, they must be given suck to, rocked in the cradle and dandled. . . . Like one lately saved from a long and dangerous sickness, and new upon his recovery, they must be forborn, spared and cherished. . . . These are the philtres charms, enticements of love by the means whereof that may be peacefully revived which was painfully acquired. Nor can a conqueror reign more happily, whether he be a monarch, emperor, king, prince or philosopher, than by making his justice to second his valour. . . . Who doth otherwise, shall not only lose what he has gained, but also be loaded with this scandal and reproach, that he is an unjust and wicked purchaser, and his acquests perish with him. . . . And although during his whole lifetime he should have peaceable possession thereof, yet if what hath been so acquired molder away in the hands of his heirs, the same opprobry, scandal and imputation will be charged upon the defunct, and his memory remain accursed for his unjust and unwarrantable conquest."

Rabelais was far-sighted. Three centuries of experience confirmed the judgment of his strange genius. Montesquieu, having considered how France acquired and retained Alsace, Roussillon, Flanders, and Franche Comté, summed up all his observations in these words: "The object of war is victory; that of victory, conquest; that of conquest, retention.—A conquest is an acquisition; the spirit of acquisition carries with it the spirit of conservation and use, not that of destruction." There was then a natural limit of conquest—the power of assimilation. Nothing should be conquered which could not be kept, and nothing should be kept which could not be absorbed. "It is the duty of a conqueror to repair some of the harm he has caused. I define the right of conquest thus: a necessary, legitimate and unhappy power which always leaves an immense debt to be paid before the account with humanity is settled." In fact, conquest legitimized itself and became a part of the law only through such a settlement. "The right of conquest, which begins with force," wrote Bossuet, "is reduced in a sense to common and natural law through the consent of peoples and peaceful possession."

It must be added that states could not expand indefinitely. They became feeble as they spread out. Too extensive frontiers complicated defense and offered an enemy too many means of attack. Besides, all size was relative. "Care must be taken that in seeking to augment the actual size, the relative is not diminished," said Montesquieu. It was often better to retain weak and divided states along one's frontiers than to conquer them and partition them with a powerful neighbor which had become an ally because of some ephemeral combination, but which always remained a rival.

The overlapping of ambitions was another limit to aggrandizement. Since there were no unclaimed lands left in Europe, no state could enrich itself except at the expense of another. But all the powers agreed in not permitting one of their number to rise above the others. Whoever pretended to the part of the lion, immediately found his rivals leaguing themselves against him. In this way a sort of partnership was formed among the great states. They intended to keep what they possessed, to divide the profits according to their investments, and to prevent any one of their associates laying down the law to the others. This is what was called the balance of power or the European equilibrium.

We find that the balance was established after great wars, when all states were weakened or ruined. Then they called a halt for a time, came to terms, and a sort of equilibrium resulted from the opposing pretensions and the limited forces. But the same causes which produced it, tended to destroy the equilibrium. Its continuation implied immobility, which was impossible. In fact, a changeless world would have required that there should be neither strong nor weak, neither misers nor prodigals, neither the indolent nor the avid, neither the capable nor the foolish. The ruin of one state or the reform of another was enough to upset the equilibrium.

"It [the balance of power] is purely a matter of opinion, which everyone interprets according to his own views or his special interests," says the instruction of a French envoy in the middle of the eighteenth century. The concept was invoked against all who aspired to supremacy: by France against the House of Hapsburg, and by England against the House of Bourbon. In the leagues which were formed, each power followed its own interest; yet while this interest often served to restrain the strong threatening states, it seldom counseled aiding the weak states which one wished to despoil. Equilibrium meant a division of forces as well as a balance between them. Counterweights were necessary. These were furnished by weak or vanquished states, while the maintenance of the balance turned inevitably to the profit of the strong, the ambitious and the capable. The rise of Prussia was the logical result of such a system. She served as a counterweight until the day when she felt strong enough to shake the diplomatic structure and upset the balance of power.

Equilibrium, then, was neither a principle of order nor a legal guarantee. Contemporaries realized this so well that they armed themselves all the more as the balance of power became more clearly defined in practice. "A new disease has spread through Europe," wrote Montesquieu. "It has attacked our princes and makes them maintain a disproportionate number of troops. . . . As soon as one state increases the number called into service, the others immediately do the same, with the result that nothing is gained thereby but the common ruin. Each monarch keeps in readiness as many armies as he would need if his people were in danger; and this condition of rivalry of all against all is called peace."

To conclude, no guarantee of peace existed other than the true understanding of individual interests, and no principle of order other than the opposition of interests. Actual practice approached the empirical rules of the following conversation. "That which is good to take is good to keep," says passion, and all the world listens.—"Nothing is worth taking which is not worth keeping," responds prudence, and very few follow its advice.—"Expansion is necessary," says ambition. "Take the strong into consideration and divide with them if they demand it, for the important thing is to control the conditions of the bargain."—"It is better," replies wisdom, "to reign among divided inferiors than to struggle for empire with powerful rivals."—"It is well to undertake only what can be achieved," concludes experience. Such calculation was the only safeguard of states against their own ambitions and against the appetites of the rest. In general we do not like to conceive of the Europe of the old regime in this way, but so it was and so it must be regarded to understand its conduct towards the French Revolution.]

VII

THE POLITICAL FOUNDATIONS have been defined; their consequences must now be studied. All were turned against the state. International law was ruined by the abuse of its own principle. There was no other penalty, but this sufficed, being both fatal and implacable. Because the state was confused with the person of the sovereign, and sovereignty was transmitted by heredity in most states, conflicts over the succession became conflicts between states. Every diplomat was paired with a lawyer. Contracts of marriage and wills became serious diplomatic questions, and, since there was no tribunal to settle resulting litigation, they were argued on the battlefield and decided by force. The reign of Louis XIV has been called one long trial, conducted with arms in the hand. The true character of the wars which occupied Europe in the eighteenth century was marked by their very names—the wars of the Spanish succession, the Austrian succession, the Bavarian succession.

As a matter of fact, no one system of law was universally respected and recognized, but there were laws which each power was ready to uphold. They were a confusion of feudal customs complicated with all the subtleties of Roman jurisprudence. What Torcy said of the Emperor Charles VI—"He regards states in which he is not master as so many usurpations against him"— could be applied to all sovereigns. Since crown lands were considered inalienable and imprescribable, law suits regarding them were always kept open. "Sovereigns never call each other into court," wrote a French publicist of the seventeenth century, "for the reason that they have no judge before whom they may plead the unjust detention of their property; they wait to regain their possessions until force is on their side. For this there is no statute of limitations, not even in a thousand years, as a bygone lawyer put it." Great princes, as Richelieu said, "considered themselves always in a position to reclaim their rights from usurpers and recover them by force." For this reason Mazarin, a foresighted man very expert in such august chicanery, wrote: "The Infanta once married to his Majesty, we will be able to aspire to the succession of the kingdoms of Spain, no matter what renunciations are made," even though the marriage of Louis XIV was then only a distant project. A century later, Frederick, judging himself in a position to secure Silesia, recalled that he had ancient rights over that province. His minister, Podewils, observed to him timidly that these rights had been annulled by solemn treaties. "Legal distinctions are the business of ministers," replied the philosopher prince; "that is your affair; the time has come to work on it secretly, for orders to the troops have already been given."

No heritage was assured and no possession was peaceful because each power kept claims suitable to it in its archives and was prepared to assert them whenever it had the opportunity. In practice even the principle of dynastic law was turned against dynasties. Princes did not stop with dispossessing heirs, they divided the inheritances. Their legal rights might not permit it, but they divided them just the same. Interested parties leagued themselves together to secure their rights. Out of this came formal contracts and partition treaties. Their terms were fixed and their validity established by the principles of equilibrium. In 1668, while the king of Spain was still living, Louis XIV partitioned his inheritance with the Emperor Leopold; in 1698 he had it redivided before an arbitration tribunal on which England and Holland had seats.

Such transactions set the tone for the diplomacy of the eighteenth century. The reason of state alone directed such devices in reality, and, with the passage of time, it was no longer concealed. Legal pretexts were relegated to the background. The partitions were destructive, and this was publicly avowed. The war of the Austrian Succession was but the loud explosion of a political order accustomed to govern itself by convenience alone. "At the death of the emperor Charles VI, the last ruler of Austria, it was believed that the day of destruction of the House of Hapsburg had come," the Duke of Choiseul wrote in an official document in 1759. "The jealousy and alarm instilled in the whole of Europe by the prodigious collection of states which the late Emperor had tried to unite under the headship of his eldest daughter; the arrangements of various princes of importance who claimed rights of succession; the separation of the imperial crown, which had been the bond of union of so many scattered states, from the House of Hapsburg by the death of the late ruler of Austria; everything, in fact, seemed to favor the design of annihilating the Empire by partitioning it. As a result of this situation, France adopted the scheme of dividing the states of the Austrian succession in conformity with the claims of the pretenders, but intermingling the parts so thoroughly that the new possessors would be continually on guard against each other's aggrandizement, and would prevent the appearance of a new power as unfriendly and as dangerous to France as the former House of Hapsburg. In this way the general peace for the future would be placed on a solid and durable foundation."

The logical development of facts and ideas led from this beginning to the supposition that the dismemberment of a state was a normal procedure of diplomacy. It was considered as a means of preventing wars by satisfying in advance the ambitions which threatened to unleash themselves, and no longer as a transaction between states with rival claims or as a necessary consequence of wars of succession. Contradictory though it may seem at first, this result was derived so directly from the principle of equilibrium that partitions were proposed at the very time when attempts were made to define this principle. The "Great Design" of Sully implied a general rearrangement of the territorial possessions of Europe. The whole structure of the treaties of Westphalia in 1648 rested on the expropriation of the ecclesiastical states for reasons of European utility. The secularizations, as they were called, set a precedent. The French Revolution found them already in the system of law, and made use of them.

There were two states—Turkey and Poland—whose geographical position and internal constitution practically destined them for such transactions. They possessed the means of satisfying everyone. The idea of dismembering them was very old and became general in the eighteenth century. In 1782 Russia and Austria agreed on the division of the Ottoman Empire after they had already, in 1772, partitioned Poland in concert with Frederick the Great because they could not then agree on the dismemberment of the Turkish Empire. The king of Prussia initiated the operation and carried it through to its conclusion but the idea came to everyone at the same time. In a sense, Poland was on the auction block of Europe, and no one had scruples against bidding according to his interests. In less than one year between the months of December, 1768, and August, 1769, the Austrian Chancellor Kaunitz proposed to Maria Theresa to buy the king of Prussia with Prussian Poland as the price; the king of Prussia claimed two Polish provinces from Russia as salary for his alliance; Russia offered them to him; the French ministry suggested a partition of Poland both at Vienna to detach Austria from Prussia and at Berlin to detach Prussia from Austria, and finally, the Turks, who were fighting in behalf of the independence of Poland, proposed to abandon their ally to Austria in order to obtain Austrian support against Russia.

In 1772 the partitioners of Poland invoked ancient rights, but such claims were only a mere form in this iniquitous act. At bottom, the powers attributed no value to them and did not expect to convince anyone. "I have a very slight opinion of our titles," avowed Maria Theresa. "The Austrians take two Polish districts," replied Catherine, "Why should not everyone take as much?" "So be it," concluded Frederick and opened the bidding. "But," he added, "when rights are not very good, they should not be set forth in detail." The declaration of 1772 subordinated these so-called rights to the following principle of convenience, the only one which could properly be invoked: "Whatever the extent or the limitations of the respective claims may be, the acquisitions which result must be exactly equal."

"This is," wrote Frederick, "the first example which history

ffords of a partition determined upon and carried through peace-
ully by three powers." It was not to be the last. After countries
ad been divided to smooth out differences, and then to prevent
nem from arising, it was to be expected that they would be
artitioned for mere convenience, and that the dismemberment of
nonarchies would become both the means and the end of states-
nanship. The weak states noted with terror the development of
practice which threatened them all. It occupied every mind
nd filled all diplomatic correspondence towards the close of the
ld regime. It was a whole system which became a part of Euro-
ean custom and which refined, completed and replaced the flexi-
le doctrine of equilibrium. It had its own name, the *copartageant*
ystem, which entered into the usage of chancelleries while wait-
ng to be given a place in the repertory of diplomacy. It had its
wn principle, which assumed false airs of legality: *acquisitions
hould be exactly equal*. It had its own false logic, which con-
used the equity of the act of division with the equality of the
arts divided and the justice of the operation with the evenness of
he balance reached, no matter whether the scales were in the
ands of judges or of thieves. It had its own jurisprudence, which,
to keep an even balance," ended by measuring the lots according
o the *fertility of the soil*, the *population*, and the *political value*,
o that it was necessary to pay attention, in the manner of the
cholastic philosophers, to the nature and quality as well as the
nere number of the population. It had its own procedure and
ormulas, which were those of shyster lawyers, such as the pledg-
ng of property to guarantee the completion of a deal. Finally,
t had its own slang, which was that of pawn brokers, such as
nargins to safeguard against fluctuations in value, and sureties to
nake good losses on loans.

It is necessary to mention these customs and explain their na-
ure, because they were in full force at the time of the French
Revolution. This was the international law which the powers
proposed to apply to France, and which, in default of submission
n her part, was applied again to Poland in 1792 and 1795.
Though revolutionary France later practiced this international

law, she did not introduce it into Europe in 1792; she did no
innovate, she imitated. Far from imposing upon the old states a
system destructive of their rights, she was forced to adopt it in
her dealings with the old states. Under these conditions she
treated with them and obtained her citizenship in Europe. By
so doing she falsified, corrupted and ruined her own principles
and the new law which she sought to have prevail; but she could
not falsify, nor corrupt, nor ruin the ancient law, for the old
Europe had already sapped its foundations. The Revolution did
not make the torrent which engulfed Europe at the end of the
century, it but added to the waters. These were facts of great
consequence, but the customs of the old regime lead to still more
serious and strange results.

VIII

WHEN FEW SCRUPLES existed against partitioning states and deposing sovereigns, there were not likely to be more against exchanging kingdoms and replacing dynasties. Nothing could have been more unstable than the state of possession in Europe at the close of the seventeenth and, even more, in the eighteenth century. The name of Alberoni, the principal minister in Spain from 1715 to 1719, is associated with this system of political rearrangements, just as that of Machiavelli is connected with that of reasons of state. Alberoni even supposed that there had been substituted "for statesmanship the caprice of a few individuals who, without rhyme or reason, perhaps for personal motives, cut and gnawed at states and kingdoms as if they were Dutch cheese."

Louis XIV's treaties for the regulation of the Spanish Succession caused a complete rearrangement of the map of Europe, a strange changing of dynasties and an astonishing migration of sovereigns and governments. According to the treaty of 1698 a Bavarian was to rule over Spain, the Indies, Belgium, and Sardinia; a Bourbon over Naples, Sicily, the Presides and Guipuzcoa; and an Austrian was to have Milan. When this combination of powers fell apart, Louis formed another in which the Bavarian disappeared, the Austrian took Spain and the Indies, and the Bourbon took Milan, which he exchanged for Lorraine, as well as taking Naples, Sicily and the Presides and exchanging them for Savoy, Nice and Piedmont. The Belgians, in the meantime, set up a republic and allied themselves with Holland so they would not be partitioned by any section of the new agreements. A treaty, drawn up almost with these terms, was signed in 1699.

The eighteenth century followed the impulse given to it. Between 1731 and 1748, Parma, where the reigning dynasty had died out, passed to Spain, then to Austria, and then returned to a younger branch of the Spanish royal house. Sardinia, assigned to Spain by the Treaty of Utrecht, was given to Austria in 1714 and to Savoy in 1720. A king of Poland obtained the succession to Lorraine, and the ruling house of Lorraine was transferred to Tuscany. Naples and Sicily, in turn separately and as a united state, experienced the most singular changes and received the most unexpected governments. The treaties of Utrecht gave Naples to Austria and Sicily to Savoy, who exchanged it in 1720 for Sardinia; then Austria reunited the two kingdoms, but they passed to the Spanish Bourbons fifteen years later.

Italy was at first the great market for kingdoms, then it was Poland, later Germany. But the movement which continued throughout the century remained the same. The French Revolution only carried it farther, while Bonaparte brought it to the logical conclusion. In a sense Europe prepared herself for conquest.

People became accustomed to such transfers, and even to the spectacle of ruined and dethroned kings wandering about the world. "Who would have believed," said Pascal, "that the king of England, the king of Poland and the queen of Sweden would be unable to find a friendly retreat and asylum in the world?" Two English kings were driven from the throne in the seventeenth century. The eighteenth century seems but a succession of quarrels between princes who contested each other's titles, dispossessed each other, expelled each other and sought to annihilate each other. No more biting satire on the manners of the time exists than the chapter of *Candide* in which Voltaire describes the strange supper his hero had in Venice, in the company of foreign kings. There was the Sultan Achmet III, who had dethroned his brother and had been dethroned by his nephew, Ivan of Russia, dethroned while in the cradle, Charles Edward, the English pretender, Augustus of Saxony and Stanislaus Leczinski, both former kings of Poland, and, to cap the climax, Theodore, king of Corsica. When they left the table, four more most serene highnesses arrived at the same hostelry. They too had lost their states by the fortune of war and had come to enjoy the rest of the carnival at Venice; but Candide paid no attention to the newcomers. All the fine people at the courts of Europe read this romance and were diverted by the macabre carnival.

If the frivolous indifference of contemporaries is astonishing, what can be said of their descendants? Voltaire was joking and exaggerating a little to suit his humor. Skip several years: the farce takes form and becomes sinister. At Erfurt in 1808, it was not the comic supper of Voltaire which might have been acted on the stage before the pit of kings which surrounded Napoleon, emperor by virtue of the Revolution. A real supper might have brought to the same table a legion of dethroned sovereigns: the Bourbon of France, the Bourbon of Spain, the Bourbon of Naples, the Braganza of Portugal, not to count bishops, grand dukes, abbots, counts and most serene highnesses.

But exile seemed a small matter; there were worse fates. "I say, 'You are Gods,' " cried Bossuet, "but, O Gods of mud and dust, you will die like men. You will fall like the great ones." They fell, indeed, but it hardly frightened those who survived. People are astonished at the lack of commotion made by the death of Louis XVI and Marie Antoinette, the lukewarm indignation, the half-hearted mourning, and the readiness with which the monarchical alliance, formed after the Revolution was stabilized, agreed to negotiate and substituted a policy of partitions for that of anti-revolutionary propaganda. After 1798 a regicide was sent as ambassador to Berlin, another to Naples and three others were accredited successively to the Holy Roman Empire at the Congress of Rastadt. The empress Marie Louise, the niece of Marie Antoinette, found several of the most famous regicides about the throne. Yet such flexibility of manners and such condescension on the part of sovereigns was far from new. If the precedents of the old regime are considered on these fine points of conduct, there is infinitely less need for surprise.

The political assassinations openly taught and practiced in the sixteenth century need not be referred to, but it is necessary to examine the sentences brought against sovereigns by the state for crimes of state by virtue of reasons of state. The case of Mary

Stuart set the precedent for modern Europe; it provided a pattern followed by all the cases which followed. Mary Stuart was a queen. She was prosecuted for acts of sovereignty by another sovereign. When, on this ground, she disputed the competence of the commission ordered to condemn her, the judge presiding over the tribunal replied: "Lay aside this vain claim of royal privilege, which cannot now save you, and plead your cause." Not content with the verdict of her commission, Queen Elizabeth had it ratified by the English parliament. Sixty-two years later, parliament applied the same law to Charles I, the grandson of Mary Stuart, placed on the throne of Elizabeth by the chances of inheritance. The question which had been raised between two sovereigns in conflict over their rights of sovereignty came up between the English nation which declared itself sovereign, and the king of England who upheld his immunities as sovereign. The scenes of the trial of Mary Stuart were repeated. "I would like to know," said Charles I, "by what power I am called here. . . . For almost a thousand years England has been an hereditary monarchy." "Sir," replied the Chancellor, "we do not sit here to reply to your questions; plead guilty or not guilty to the accusation." These two statements sum up the trial of Louis XVI in 1792.

It may be asked what princes did when faced with these attacks on the majesty of royalty. Henry III sought to intervene in favor of Mary Stuart; she had been queen of France. He sent to London the statement that he resented her condemnation as "a thing contrary to the common interest of all kings." When Elizabeth paid no attention, Henry III did not insist. Philip of Spain, the enemy of England, sought to avenge the queen of Scotland. Elizabeth defeated him. Some years later, the ally of Henry IV of France, respected or feared by all monarchs, Elizabeth peacefully left her crown to the son of her victim. It might be said that this was only a quarrel among rulers, that royalty itself was not in question. But when Charles I was concerned, the trial was held between a legitimate sovereign and a people in revolt, and the solution was identical.

Europe was moved by the death of the king of England in

1649, but each power showed its feelings only to the extent that they agreed with its interests. Holland, a republic, was the most indignant, together with Russia, subject to a barbarous despotism. Holland was in open rivalry with England; the Tsar of Muscovy had nothing to lose and did not fear England. Spain and France, on the other hand, after protesting lightly against the execution of the king, competed to be the first to recognize the Commonwealth. In vain it was alleged that Charles I had reigned by the same title as Louis XIV, that the queen was a daughter of France, that the revolution which overthrew the English throne menaced all thrones. Nothing prevailed against the fact that the Commonwealth was strong and that it was to the interest of France to come to an understanding with it. The implacable realism of the reason of state prevailed over all emotions based on honor, religion, and established law. "If we were ruled by considerations of law and justice," wrote Mazarin to the regent, Anne of Austria, "the Commonwealth ought not to be recognized. Nothing could be more prejudicial to the reputation of the King than a recognition by which he abandons the interests of a legitimate monarch, near-relation, neighbor and ally, and nothing could be more unjust than to recognize usurpers who have stained their hands with the blood of their sovereign. . . . But since the laws of honor and justice must not be placed above the counsels of prudence, we must admit . . . that a continued refusal to recognize the Commonwealth will neither increase nor confirm the rights of the Stuarts. . . . Besides, there is reason to fear that, if the Spaniards are once more closely joined to the English, the latter will not come to a settlement with us, and, if they do not actually make war upon us, will at least give the Spanish most important assistance against us. There remains no room for doubt, then, that we should enter into negotiations with the Commonwealth of England without delay and grant the recognition it desires." Louis XIV recognized the Commonwealth, and all Europe did likewise.

"What times, what ways are these!" cried La Bruyère. "O unfortunate age, an age filled with bad examples. . . . A man says:

'I will cross the sea, I will despoil my father of his patrimony, I will drive him, his wife, and his heir from his lands and from his states'; and his actions conform to his words. He ought to fear the anger of the various kings whom he outrages in the person of one king alone. But they tolerate him, they almost say: 'Cross the sea, despoil your father, demonstrate to the whole world that it is possible to drive a king from his kingdom like a petty noble from his castle or a tenant from his holding!' . . . Royal dignity has no more privileges, kings themselves have renounced them!'" These were the words of an eloquent pessimist, not of a statesman. To the latter, royal dignity was sacred only for dreamers and theologians. Statesmanship had no care but for security and self-interest. No law protected majesty against passion. In 1689 the soldiers of Louis XIV sacked the cathedral at Spires, in which were the tombs of eight emperors. Their ashes were thrown to the winds because Louvois wished to terrify and disgrace the Germans.

There was even no fear of unchaining popular fury and the blind fanaticism of mobs. In 1691 the rumor spread in Paris that William III of England had just died. "Everyone," wrote Louvois, "woke his friends, bonfires were lighted without permits, and much wine was consumed." The confused police sought to calm the effervescence, but the people surrounded the policemen, embraced them and dragged them into the dance. The movement spread to the provinces. Everywhere a "mad and furious" people celebrated the death of the enemy. It was the revolutionary carmagnole in anticipation, and, what was more serious, it was a carmagnole for which a royal death provided the impulse. The words of Louvois might have been written in the following century, among the *sans-culottes*. "For several days and nights, one had the pleasure of seeing effigies of William and Mary hanged, quartered, branded by butchers, dragged through the streets, led on donkeys with outrageous inscriptions, or torn to pieces by students of the Jesuits dressed like demons. The galleries of the Saint Innocent cemetery were filled with prints of the two sovereigns in all sorts of scandalous postures. Enormous quantities of wine, at good prices, were drunk to the confusion of the defunct; cries loud enough to pierce the air were raised against the English king." So the people of Paris, in the reign of a prince called by Bossuet "the invincible defender and immediate avenger of violated majesty," interpreted the principles of the reason of state with the passive approval of the police. Paris learned that kings could commit crimes, that they could be judged and that a traitor or an enemy king ceased to be a king. With the idea of sovereignty displaced, the logical conclusion was for the people to turn next against their own king these precedents set by royalty. The king of France would become the usurper, the traitor, the archenemy. A straight incline led men down to the revolutionary events of 1793.

The eighteenth century followed this downward path with frivolous cynicism. The reason of state no longer commanded men with the brutal conciseness of the preceding century; it discussed, it dissertated, it sought elegant sophism and was proud of its fine style. In 1718 the Tsar Peter had his son beheaded for a crime of state. Several moralists considered protesting. Voltaire reminded them of order, history, the principles of the Roman law and the rules of classical tragedy, which the thinkers of the time confused so willingly. "Peter was more king than father, he sacrificed his own son to his interests as a founder of the state and as a law maker. . . . If Alexis had ascended the throne, all would have been ruined. . . . When this catastrophe of a son's death is considered, sensitive hearts may shudder but firm ones approve."

When necessary, the reason of state could become amiable and speak with grace. In 1742 Elizabeth Petrovna raised the Russian guards, marched at their head into the palace, and imprisoned the regent. The Tsar Ivan was a child of two. In pity she took him into her arms and embraced him. Then, having made this concession to "sensitive hearts," she sought the counsel of "strong minds," particularly the French Ambassador, the Marquis de la Chétardie. He was young, tender, and emotional; he represented in the rough Russian court the refinement of western Europe. Elizabeth had taken him as her lover, and he had aided her greatly in securing the throne. The Marquis wrote: "Too much cannot be done to efface even the traces of Ivan VI. By this means alone can Russia be secured permanently against the evils which circumstances may occasion and which the example of the false Demetrius should cause particularly to be apprehended in this country." The advice was given in most polite terms, but the hypocrisy in the form showed all the more the cruelty in the thought. Elizabeth recoiled before such an extreme measure; she had the child shut up in a fortress where he languished twenty-three years and died. In revolutionary France Louis XVII died sooner. He was less robust, but was nevertheless subjected to the same law. In spite of the poignancy of his fate, in spite of the circumstances which made this atrocious sequestration of a child an historical event, his imprisonment and death produced hardly more effect than that of the unfortunate Ivan, like him a victim of the same reason of state.

More and more the world became accustomed to the reason of state. Russia greatly enriched the store of precedents, but the barbarous customs of a barbarous state are not so astonishing as the indifference with which the governments of old Europe watched the spectacle. In 1762, Catherine, a German princess married to the Tsar Peter III, plotted to upset the throne. The Tsar was arrested, deposed and assassinated in his prison. Diplomats reported this deed as the most natural thing in the world. They were neither scandalized nor moved; some were even overjoyed because they supposed the change would benefit their courts. Among their number was the Count de Mercy, ambassador to Maria Theresa, who later resided a long time in Paris, where he played an important role at the outbreak of the revolution. He describes the incident, concluding: "Such has been the course of one of the greatest and most joyful events which has ever taken place. . . . The nation was exasperated against Peter III, and nothing was required but to learn how to put an end to his insensate rule." Bérenger, a Frenchman who was only a chargé d'affaires, alone gave in to a few considerations of morality and philosophy. "What a spectacle!" he wrote, "On the one side the grandson of Peter I dethroned and put to death, on the other the [great] grandson of Tsar Ivan V languishing in irons, while a princess of Anhalt usurps the crown of their ancestors, preparing the way to the throne by a regicide!"

The agents of the crime revealed the fact; governments judged it according to their convenience. For Frederick the Great of Prussia, who had been barely saved from disaster by the friendship of Peter III, it was a "thunder bolt"; for Maria Theresa, who had been abandoned by Peter III, it was a stroke of fortune. "I bow before the divine Providence which has watched over Austria, the Russian empire and Christianity," she wrote to Mercy. "Never has news gladdened my heart as much as this fortunate accession to the throne." The English "cordially congratulated" the new tsarina. As for Louis XV, who supposed he had reason to rejoice for the same cause as his ally, Maria Theresa—he did not restrain expressions of admiration and instructed his ambassador, Baron de Breteuil, as follows: "The dissimulation of the empress and her courage at the moment of execution of her project indicate a princess capable of conceiving and executing great deeds. I am struck with the eagerness with which not only courtiers but even foreigners and all the ministers near this princess seek to pay their respects to her and even to attract special attention so as to attach Rusia more intimately to the interests of their masters. The respect due to crowned heads should guide your conduct and your conversations with the Empress." This respect, it seems, was not owed to heads from which the crowns had been taken. The story of the rise of Catherine was soon known. Rulhière told it in a work appearing in 1773. He concealed nothing, neither the conspiracy of the tsarina nor her intrigues nor her amours. The book attracted attention; Catherine wished to read it and asked about it of Diderot, who happened to be in her presence. The philosopher, who prided himself on effrontery, nevertheless took several oratorical precautions. "As to that which concerns you, Madam," said he, "this work is a satire against you if you make much of goodness and virtue, outworn garments of your sex; but if large views and manly, patriotic ideals interest you more, the author depicts you as a great princess, and, everything considered, does you more honor than harm." "You make me all the more eager to read this work," replied the tsarina.

Fundamentally, relations between sovereigns were based on self-interest while outwardly they adhered to the forms of good breeding. This sometimes led to delicate situations, and required singular vigilance. Thus, in 1781, the Grand Duke Paul of Russia, the heir if not the legitimate son of Peter III, went to Vienna, where he was magnificently received. Gala fetes were arranged. At the opera, *Orestes* was to be presented, accompanied by a ballet; at the theatre, *Hamlet* was prepared. In spite of the music and the dancing, *Orestes* lent itself impertinent allusions, while *Hamlet* passed all bounds. The actor Schroeder called attention to this, and people were so delighted to have avoided, thanks to him, such a gross impropriety, that he was rewarded for his tact with a present of fifty ducats. The precaution was all the more necessary because the grand duke had an uneasy conscience and was constantly troubled by ghosts like those of the prince of Denmark. Several years later a French agent wrote, "This prince follows in all respects the path of his unfortunate father, and, unless the heart of the grand duchess is a temple of all the virtues, will one day experience the same fate as Peter III. He expects it, and even says so to the grand duchess herself. The circumstances of his murder in 1801, and the manner in which the news was received in Europe, demonstrate that traditions regarding such matters had not changed either in Russia or in the old courts of Europe in spite of the catastrophe of 1793.

IX

THE CONDUCT OF SOVEREIGNS faced with attacks on the persons of sovereigns explains the conduct of governments faced with attacks against governments, or revolutions. There had been many in Europe, but no one imagined that the idea of revolution could be abstract from the particular circumstances under which the different revolutions had been produced. Revolution by itself, considered as a normal and continual overthrowing of societies, was a notion as strange to the statesmen of the old regime as that of dynastic legitimacy, considered as the immutable and absolute principle of sovereignty. These two quite abstract conceptions were formed simultaneously in the course of the French revolution as a result of identical philosophical methods. As Joseph de Maistre wrote in 1796, the French revolution was "an event unique in history." It was for this reason that men of the old regime were so completely mistaken regarding the character of the revolution. They judged it by the precedents, and conducted themselves accordingly.

The men of the old regime knew from history and had seen for themselves many outbreaks produced by eternal misery, irritations, brutal greed, factious excitement, criminal conspiracies—in short, the anarchy arising spontaneously when government becomes too evil or when authority is relaxed. They had witnessed "those upheavals to which peoples are naturally disposed." They had followed their course in the Italian republics; they knew the violence of factions and the methods employed by them—exile, confiscation, death, sedition, civil war. They had seen the same events, with the same results in France and England. They knew also that man when left to his own resources reverted to a ferocious savage, as stupid and confused as nature had originally made him. All this was known, and it all seemed very simple. Revolts were but the chronic disease of states, the natural form of their decadence and death. The cause of the illness was to be found in the states themselves—the wearing out of the vital organs through old age or excesses, not a wound or a contagion from the outside. "Political bodies," wrote Pasquier, one of the most observant of the old historians, "are formed, grow, and come to an end according to fixed rules. . . . Nothing is more natural than dissolution caused by the enfeeblement of the forces which had previously produced growth." Bossuet boldly placed responsibility upon governments. "However far one searches through history for examples of great changes, one finds that up to now they have always been caused either by the softness or the violence of princes. In fact, when princes neglect their finances and their armies, neither keep the laws nor a sense of measure and are no longer respected and feared by their subjects, making the evils of the present seem worse than anything the future might hold, then ruling houses are fearfully menaced by excessive license or patience pushed to extremes."

This being the case, governments regarded revolution in a foreign state as only a local problem, and judged it according to their interests. They stimulated or calmed the revolution according to whether it was advantageous to support the state involved, or else to weaken it. This was a favorite political maneuver, a classic resource of diplomacy.

The great religious revolution which shook central Europe in the sixteenth century, and which kept it in a state of war until the middle of the seventeenth century, was remembered by statesmen as the greatest opportunity which history had afforded them. It was an age of iron virtues, perhaps, but it was also an age with a tendency for political negotiation and war. The wealth of political opportunities in the age was as celebrated as the mines of Peru, where whole generations were sacrificed to fill a few Spanish galleons with gold. The actual character of the religious revolution escaped governments because they were concerned only with its results, just as in the case of the French revolution, two hundred years later. Like the political and social revolution of the eighteenth century, the religious revolution of the sixteenth was abstract in principle and cosmopolitan in action. It proceeded from universal ideas, and appealed to all peoples. It drew together those who had been divided, and divided those who had been united. It provoked struggles and forged alliances between governments. It fomented seditions and brought on civil wars. It produced its own apostles, proselytes, martyrs and fanatics. It upset the whole of Europe, and then fused together again its constituent elements. Yet this chaos was only on the surface; when the crisis abated, all the elements were arranged according to their natural affinities.

The Reformation addressed itself to all nations, and each interpreted the movement according to its own tendencies, particular traditions and acquired ideas. It stimulated and even over-excited national passions; it furnished them with a new form and new energy; but it did not create them. Thus in Germany the Reformation caused the antagonism between north and south to burst into war, while in England it was associated with the establishment of free government. In France it appeared, according to circumstances, as both an aristocratic and a republican movement, serving as a pretext for the pretensions of the nobles against royalty and of the people against the nobles.

Nations adapted the Reformation to their traditions, and governments to their systems. Spain and France were in open rivalry. Spain profited by the wars of religion to excite sedition in France; she supported fanaticism and subsidized demagogy. The French sought to create a diversion in Germany. There the house of Austria fought the Reformation in the name of political unity, while the German princes supported it because they wished disunion. Austria claimed universal monarchy, but could obtain it only through unity of faith and with the support of the Roman church. The Austrian emperor Charles V and his son Philip II of Spain remained Catholic to the end. The king of France opposed Austrian domination. He supported the reformers in Germany and made himself the champion of German liberties. These liberties were intimately linked with the success of the

Reformation, for the German princes who adopted the new movement hoped to become independent of the Emperor and the Empire. The king of France, who did his best to help them, nevertheless repressed the Reformation in his own dominions because he wished to be master there, and because the nobles sought to use it against him just as the princes of the Empire used it against the house of Austria. Thus the great religious crisis was transformed into a political crisis; conflicts of power superseded conflicts of principle, and the struggle ended with a redistribution of territory.

The essentially wordly and political character of the treaties of Westphalia demonstrates the attitude of European governments towards the Reformation. The treaties contributed, no doubt, to the establishment of liberty of conscience, but they did so very indirectly, and by the force of circumstance rather than the design of man. In the famous maxim "Cuius regio, eius religio" (to each part, its own religion), it was the religion of the state which prevailed. In other words, the reason of state was applied to matters of conscience, a condition much nearer intolerance than liberty. The transaction between the states was made on the principle that each was confirmed in its own independence and that the large expanded at the expense of the small. To obtain peace, the Catholic states which represented the old order made a composition with the new order and consented to the secularization of church property. The public law of the middle ages was violated in principle and action; unity of faith and the supremacy of the Pope disappeared along with the petty feudal principalities which were absorbed by the larger states. If the treaties of 1648 are compared with the Napoleonic reorganizations of Germany in 1801 and 1803, one is forced to conclude that the former inflicted as deep a wound upon the public law of the old Europe as the latter, which were but a consequence and an imitation of the treaties of Westphalia. When the governments of the close of the eighteenth century were faced with the French revolution, so like the Reformation in its political consequences, they conducted themselves like the governments of the sixteenth century. The jurisprudence of the old regime in revolutionary matters came from the famous precedents of the age of the Reformation.

Intervention in civil wars was the first and most fruitful application of these precedents. The civil wars which succeeded the private wars of the feudal regime were similar to them in character. The feudal regime, in which the suzerain stood in place of the country and in which the state was divided and sovereignty was confused, permitted the greatest latitude in the making of alliances. The barons, fighting among themselves or against their overlords, had no scruples against seeking aid from other barons or even other overlords. This custom was perpetuated wherever the feudal system remained, as in Germany, and was sanctioned by the treaties of Westphalia. In France, where royal authority prevailed over feudal power, the custom survived the circumstances which had given it birth. The usages followed in the feudal struggle were applied in the struggles sustained against the sovereign state. Factions brought in foreign support, and each believed itself to be within its rights, because each pretended to be the state itself, and to outweigh all the others. Believing itself the state, each faction also believed itself the nation, confusing the two concepts. Richelieu fought both the Huguenots and the English at La Rochelle; Mazarin had to fight a coalition of Spaniards and French Frondeurs. The illustrious failings of two heroes of the century are well known. Turenne and Condé, who achieved the most for France against the foreigner, became in turn allies of the foreigner against the French state.

Without a doubt, the concepts of sovereignty, the state, and the country tended to be separated, defined, and made precise. In the sixteenth century Bodin wrote: "There is never a just cause for taking arms against the prince or the country." High treason became a more clearly defined crime and was punished more regularly. Nevertheless the attitudes common in the wars of the sixteenth century and the wars of the Fronde had by no means disappeared in the age of the French revolution. When similar conditions occurred, the old attitudes reappeared spontaneously.

No other origin can be assigned to the emigration of French nobles, who armed and allied themselves with the coalition against
France. This was the final episode of feudal polity, coinciding
with the disappearance of the last vestiges of feudalism.

At this moment, as the effect of the armed emigration, the
separation was permanently made between the concepts of the
country and of the prince. Doubtless this separation, one of the
principal phenomena of the French revolution, was prepared be-
forehand, even by royalty itself. But it was not consummated in
all minds, and particularly not in the minds of the nobles against
whom it was directed and who claimed as their own precisely
these feudal customs. In this way the armed emigration could
take place, which organized a new state against the state, contracted alliances, and invaded French territory in the midst of
foreign armies. The emigrant nobles considered that they were
exercising a right because they claimed to be the state and the
country and to fight only against usurpers.

Such a state of mind was general in Europe, and governments
profited by using it against each other. Not content with en-
couraging factions, they excited them. Insead of merely supporting civil war, they provoked it; instead of exploiting revolutions,
they prepared them. "Is it prudent and just to wait until the
others are devoured in order to be the last," wrote Richelieu. A
contemporary apology for Louis XIV reads: "Though it may be
shameful for a prince to foment the rebellion of subjects against
their legitimate prince, the House of Hapsburg long ago showed
us the way. . . . If it is the established usage for sovereigns to in-
jure each other as much as possible, why attribute to us a fault
which the whole world shares with us?" In fact each country
prided itself, according to Saint Simon, on contriving strange
revolutions among the others. The English never lost an opportunity against Louis XIII and Louis XIV, who returned the favor
with interest. The latter thought it expedient to encourage sedition wherever he had enemies. He wrote in his *Memoirs*: "I kept
up certain contacts in Hungary in order to start trouble for the
Emperor whenever he might wish to concern himself with my

affairs." But the most striking example and the most characteristic precedent was that of the relations between the courts of France and England during the rebellions of the seventeenth century. They illustrated in advance the shifts in the policies of the great powers, such as Austria, towards France during the revolution.

Charles I of England fought for the royal prerogative, and the French monarchy was carrying on the same struggle at the same time. If the revolutionary party triumphed in England, the party of factions in France would naturally be encouraged. The government was not moved by this consideration. "The situation seems very favorable for embarrassing the king of England," wrote the ambassador of Louis XIII in 1637. Richelieu did not miss it. While he was pushing on the disaffected party, he secretly encouraged the Court. When Queen Henrietta Maria wished to take refuge in France, he dissuaded her. "On such occasions, whoever breaks off the battle, loses it," he instructed her. What he wished was disorder in the state, and the consequent weakening of England.

Mazarin's policy was no different. His agents, d'Harcourt in 1644, and Bellièvre in 1647, were instructed to keep things stirred up. Parliament declared itself sovereign in Great Britain. Mazarin thought "that it was not a time for disputing over formalities," and recognized the sovereignty of parliament. Queen Henrietta Maria, sister of the king of France, felt herself abandoned, betrayed; she wept and raged against this perfidious policy. Yet the time came when the English revolution seemed to threaten even the continent. As Bossuet warned, the sectarian spirit appeared, "the seditious dream of independent and impious and sacrilegious delusion which leads them to destroy all monarchies and equalize all men." France was in open civil war. The Frondeurs used the example and boasted of the support of the British Commonwealth. The Commonwealth threatened to spread to the outside world the ardent flame which was consuming it from within. It was credited with the design of annexing Holland, which had a similar government and religion. "Let us make them one people with us," wrote an envoy of parliament in Holland. The English became arrogant. "I will make the name of the English as great as that of the Romans," said Cromwell. He meditated a league of all the protestant powers, under his direction. It was announced that he would cross to France at the head of his army. The statement was ascribed to him that "had he been ten years younger, there would be no king in Europe whom he would not cause to tremble, and, having a better motive than the late king of Sweden [Charles XII], he believed himself capable of accomplishing even more for the good of peoples than the former had ever done by his ambition."

Warned and threatened, Mazarin, it might seem, should have hastened to form a counterleague. He did just the opposite. Since Cromwell and the Commonwealth took such a firm stand, he judged it better to have them as friends than as enemies. He proposed an agreement with them, and they accepted because it was to their interests. The Most Christian King became the ally of a protestant and regicide republic, and this republic made war on Holland, the only continental state with a similar religion and government. "I will not recount," cried Bossuet, "the too fortunate conclusion of his enterprises, nor his famous victories by which virtue was outraged, nor our long tranquillity which astonished the universe." No astonishment was warranted. If the successes of Cromwell were inexplicable in some quarters, they were not at the court of Louis XIV The greatest of kings did not hesitate to call Cromwell a "prince" and to declare that he "considered him one of the greatest and most happy in Europe."

Cromwell's prestige throughout Europe was immense. In going over his career, one seems to be reading a brief anticipation of that of Bonaparte. He was feared, he was admired, he was sought after. He received ambassadors from Sweden, Germany, Italy and even from Poland. The prince of Condé wrote to him in 1653: "I consider the people of the United Kingdom to have reached the pinnacle of happiness now that their possessions and lives are confided to the leadership of such a great man. As for me, I entreat Your Highness to believe that I would consider

myself most fortunate to be able to serve you in any manner."
The admiration which Cromwell inspired survived his power.
Though he was dead and the Commonwealth overthrown, this
phrase appears in the *Memoirs* of Louis XIV for 1662: "Cromwell, in whom genius, opportunity and the misfortune of his
country had inspired thoughts far above his birth."

While ambassadors flocked about the Protector in London,
Charles II, the legitimate heir to the English throne, proscribed
and miserable, wandered from city to city on the continent beg-
ging a secret audience for his envoys, food for his servants, and
asylum for himself and his followers. Embarrassing people everywhere and being turned out everywhere, he received only hidden condolences and public affronts. His experience was a preface to the history of the Bourbons from the Revolution to 1814.
Then Charles II reascended the throne. Bossuet gloried in it to
Louis XIV. "The injury to kings has been avenged," he cried,
but Louis XIV was not dazzled enough to forget the traditions
of his policy. One reads in his *Memoirs* for 1666: "I maintained
pensioners in Ireland to raise up the Catholics there against the
English, and I entered into relations with certain refugees from
England to whom I promised large sums in order to revive the
remnants of the faction of Cromwell."

If he acted in this way towards Charles II, a legitimate sovereign, his protegé of but the day before and still in his pay, he
acted even more freely towards William III, a usurping sovereign
and the most inveterate of his enemies. The spirit to which the
eighteenth century conformed is accurately revealed in this note
of 1666.

X

THERE WERE MANY REVOLUTIONS in the eighteenth century, but there was no connection between them. Neither was there the slightest relationship between the forms of governments and their conduct towards each other in these periods of crisis. Each pursued its own immediate interest, the conduct of policy changing everywhere with circumstances. To the French, and in general to statesmen on the continent, England appeared as a country torn by factions. "The government of this island is more stormy than the sea which surrounds it," said Voltaire. What was only a sedition in other countries was a revolution in England. Diplomats depicted the country as always on the verge of revolution. The politicians of Versailles congratulated themselves on it. "We are not eager," wrote M. de Choiseul, "to see a strong ministry established in England. I hope that anarchy will not cease to be imminent. I would like to have it continue for a century." In 1762 the rumor spread that the boyars of Russia wished to imitate the magnates of Poland and form a sort of royal republic. Louis XV was then in a bad humor against Russia. He wrote to his ambassador, "Everything which may plunge it into chaos and cause it to return to obscurity is advantageous to my interests."

For this reason the neighbors of Poland showed themselves such jealous guardians of the liberties which kept this republic in anarchy and prepared the way for interventions and partitions. With its anachronistic constitution, Poland repeated the confused and somber chronicle of the wars of the middle ages in the Europe of the eighteenth century. Every faction invoked foreign aid; every foreign power supported a faction. It was a matter of principle at Vienna, Petersburg and Berlin to oppose at all costs every reform which tended to strengthen the Polish state. The constitution even permitted neighboring powers to foment trouble, and disorders then served as a pretext for intervening in the affairs of the republic and completing its ruin. Thus a civil war was fomented in 1768, and in 1772 the neighboring states declared it right and necessary to dismember Poland to put an end to the anarchy which had become established and which threatened their interests.

The Swedish constitution resembled in some respects that of Poland. While it did not offer simple opportunities to the neighbors of Sweden, it seemed a matter of interest to them, and they supported it strongly. The enemies of Sweden spoke of Swedish liberties with the dignified tone of the Roman senate. The instructions given to the minister of Denmark at Stockholm in 1767 read: "Every power and every man supporting Swedish liberties and laws has a claim upon the friendship, cooperation, and support of the Danish king, every power which attacks them is his enemy, and every man who opposes them is disgraced in his eyes."

When the precious liberties of Sweden seemed in danger, Frederick the Great displayed a "generosity" which would have surprised Lafayette, and Catherine the Great a "virtue" sufficient to disconcert Madame Roland. In 1764 and 1769, these two despots formally engaged themselves to oppose in Sweden "the re-establishment of sovereignty." Gustavus III of Sweden proposed to re-establish it, and France, needing an ally in the north, aided him. He carried out a *coup d'etat* which, without any doubt, saved the Swedes from the fate of Poland, He received encouragement from Versailles, threats from Petersburg and Berlin. This ruler, who restored royal power, was forced to excuse himself to neighboring rulers. If we consider the terms of his apology, we may well ask what the cause of monarchy was worth when a king was forced to defend it before other kings in these terms: "Tell me in the name of God," wrote Gustavus III to his uncle Prince Henry of Prussia, Frederick's brother, "tell me what I have done to draw down upon myself the storm by which you state I am so certainly threatened. Have I not manifested my peaceful intentions in the most evident manner? If it is a question of the change made in the form of government of my kingdom, you are too fair not to realize that this is a matter which cannot be discussed with foreign powers. It was achieved and ratified by the Swedish nation, and this nation thinks itself fortunate. What right then can foreign rulers have to seek a quarrel with me for having rendered my subjects happy? If this be a cause for war, there is no more justice in the world. . . . What will I gain from treaties and guarantees by powers which do not recognize any law but their own will, and consider only the forces at their disposal in executing them? It is incredible that I should be attacked in defiance of all principles of law and justice and that the rights of all sovereigns and all independent nations should at the same time be placed in jeopardy."

A nation which had freed itself would not have used different arguments to justify its independence. The fact is that no one cared whether the purpose of a revolution was to establish the liberty of a people or the power of a sovereign. The same attitude was taken towards a democratic revolution and a royal *coup d'etat*. Thus, at the same time that she favored the party of the king in Sweden and in Poland and would have liked to support the aristocracy against royalty in Russia, France supported in America the people of the colonies in revolt against England. This war was not ended before the same king and the same minister, Louis XVI and the Count of Vergennes, intervened in Geneva against the democratic party. France would have found it most difficult to establish any relation in principle between these opposite policies. The truth of the matter was that she had no principle other than the interest of the state, and that seemed sufficient. "The insurgents whom I am driving from Geneva are the agents of England," wrote Vergennes, "while the American insurgents are our friends for years to come. I have dealt with them both, not by reason of their political systems, but by reason of their attitude towards France. Such are my reasons of state."

All political thinking was, in fact, based on such considerations. A new example soon occurred, the last and one of the most significant in the history of the old regime. In 1787 revolts which were almost revolutions broke out in the Austrian Netherlands and in the United Netherlands—that is, in Belgium and in Holland. In Belgium the aristocracy, supported by the Catholic clergy, demanded the preservation of old franchises destroyed or threatened by the centralizing government of the Emperor Joseph II. In Holland the democrats and patriots armed themselves against the Statholder who was intriguing for some form of dictatorship and looking forward to taking over the republic. In both countries peoples were defending their national liberties and rulers were seeking absolute power.

The conduct of the large states in this situation demonstrated perfectly the extent to which all Europe lacked consistent principles. France upheld, tacitly in Belgium and openly in Holland, the party of freedom, which was the party she had opposed in Sweden. England, which had just been fighting her rebellious subjects in America, favored the Belgians revolting against Austria but energetically took the side of the Statholder against his Dutch subjects. Thus the absolute monarchy which reigned at Versailles demanded their national liberties for these peoples, while the limited monarchy which governed England helped an ambitious ruler in Holland to destroy these liberties. Joseph II of Austria and his minister Kaunitz, who looked with approbation upon the anarchy in Poland, sought to take from the Belgians the liberties which they judged so precious to the Poles. The Prussians, finally, who were inciting and sustaining the revolution in Belgium, intervened with an army to crush the one in Holland, and established there the sort of strong government which they did not wish to see either in Stockholm or in Warsaw or in Brussels.

In the whole of the eighteenth century, I find but one league formed among crowned heads for the purpose of intervention, and it was directed against royal authority. This was the league of the northern powers against Poland and Sweden. As for the powers of western and southern Europe, I find but one case in which they pursued in concert a common object. This was the suppression of the Jesuit order. The incident is characteristic. It appears as a sort of bas-relief, in which the political customs of the times are revealed in a few striking traits. Both the Bourbons and the Braganzas, that is, France, Spain, Naples, Parma and Portugal, had driven the Jesuits from their respective states for purely political reasons. The rulers were able to act in the fullness of their sovereignty because there was no established constitution or declared public law in any of these governments which limited their absolute power in such a case. But it was not enough to expel the Jesuits if they reassembled elsewhere. It was necessary to close every land of refuge to them, and even destroy the order itself. Its existence depended upon the Pope, the most feeble of the sovereigns of the continent. The stronger sovereigns did not hesitate to form a coalition to force him to submit to their will. They required of the Pope only the use of his spiritual power; it followed that, if they had any respect for the rights of the Church, they should use no other means but persuasion. Their representations should have been reserved and deferent, as was proper in addressing themselves to the Holy Father who had honored them with the titles "Most Faithful King," "Catholic King" and "Most Christian King."

To expect such consideration and such delicacy from rulers would show little understanding of the manners of the time. Their demands were pressing, haughty, arrogant. What is more, they were accompanied by threats and upheld by force. Pope though he might be, Clement XIII was but another sovereign, and the most defenseless of all. He was treated accordingly. Since the Pope was vested with sovereignty of a double character, the usurpation was double. The temporal sovereign was required to close his frontiers against a proscribed order, the spiritual sovereign to suppress it. It was an impious attack upon both the temporal and spiritual power. They did not stop at this, however. The two powers being joined, the one was used in the attack on the other. Because the temporal power of the papacy was most easily reached, the sovereigns laid siege to the spiritual power through it, and hoped in this way to force its capitulation. The Church being a state, it came under the law of states, which meant that it ceased to be inviolable. The powers in coalition against the Jesuits acted towards the Holy See as Louis XIV would have acted towards the republic of Holland after the revocation of the Edict of Nantes if the proscribed protestants had had no other refuge and if the Dutch had had neither an army nor allies to defend themselves.

Clement XIII sought to resist. The Spanish Bourbon Duke of Parma, the weakest but not the least enterprising of the allies, was in his power as a result of difficulties in his Italian territories. The Duke had reformed their ecclesiastical laws and contested the suzerainty which the Holy See claimed over them. By virtue of this suzerainty the Pope, in a note dated January 30, 1768, declared the decrees of the Duke null and void and summoned him to retract them under pain of excommunication. The Bourbon king of France replied to this usurpation of the rights of a prince of his own house by the occupation of the papal territories of Avignon and the County of Orange, and the Bourbon king of Naples by the occupation of Benevento and Ponte Corvo, and a claim of sovereignty over these lands in addition. Then, in identical notes sent to the Holy See in January, 1769, France, Naples and Spain demanded of the Pope the suppression of the Jesuits. Clement XIII died several days later. The allies busied themselves in arranging the selection of his successor. "If the new pope should follow the principles of Clement XIII," wrote Choiseul, "the kings will do of their own accord by force that which they ask the Holy Father to do out of good will."

Cardinal Ganganelli promised to suppress the Jesuits, and became pope under the name of Clement XIV. Then he sought to gain time. He struggled for more than four years, but the allies held firm and yielded nothing on the point at issue. "The King," wrote the French minister d'Aiguillon on January 11, 1773, "has seized this state—Avignon—only because the House of Bourbon was angered at the proceedings of the late pope aganst the Duke of Parma, and has retained it only because the king of Spain requested him to defer restitution until he should have satisfaction in the affair of the Jesuits. As soon as he shall have attained it, the

King will return Avignon." The ambassador of Louis XV at Rome, the Cardinal de Bernis, replied on February 17, "It is besides most desirable for France always to have at hand a sure means of putting the court of Rome back on the right course if it should happen to stray from it. Avignon can be taken when wanted, and Rome will always be influenced by this possibility." Naples followed the same policy, and the restitution of Benevento, like that of Avignon, depended in reality on the suppression of the Jesuits. The Pope capitulated, the Jesuits were suppressed, and the Holy See recovered its domains.

It is necessary to follow the strange affair of the Jesuits to its conclusion in order to show completely the skepticism of the old Europe and the anarchy of the Christian Republic. While the Catholic governments were proscribing the Jesuits and usurping the authority of the Pope, heretics and schismatics received the proscribed order and prided themselves on being more papist than the Holy See. Frederick needed teachers for his Roman Catholic subjects in Prussia. It was a good opportunity to secure them at little expense and he profited by it. He said to the Prince de Ligne: "Since my brothers, the Catholic, the Most Christian and the Most Faithful and Apostolic kings have driven them out, I, the most heretical, gather in as many as I can." He had no fear of the Jesuits; scattered among a protestant population and regimented with Prussian functionaries, they were necessarily obedient. "I know well enough," he wrote to Voltaire, "that they have formed factions and meddled in politics, but such things are the fault of the government. Why should it permit them?" The Great Catherine imitated her neighbor and, like him, felt that she had done well. The Fathers, who had proved so unaccommodating towards catholic governments, became most pliable and submissive in the hands of these two despots, who were more free thinkers than protestants. For example, after the partition of Poland in 1772, they preached to the annexed Poles that they should submit to the orthodox tsarina and to the Lutheran king of Prussia.

In view of these facts, I conclude that if anything seemed improbable at the close of the old regime and even contradictory to established custom, it was a coalition founded on international law for the defense of this law. In the words of Frederick, "A Pope who would have wanted to preach a crusade could not have assembled twenty blackguards." A Holy Alliance before 1788 would have been a veritable historical paradox. The old Europe was incapable of such a thing, and the French revolution was required to bring it into being.

XI

DIPLOMACY IS THE EXPRESSION of political customs. The diplomats of the old regime formed, in the most brilliant society of Europe, a particularly exquisite and refined group. Yet it is not the purpose of this study to deal with the spirit, the methods or the language of diplomacy, but with fundamentals—that is, with the points of view and the actions which must be considered to understand how this diplomacy could be so easily adapted to revolutionary purposes and how the men of the revolution could appropriate its procedures with such facility.

The negotiations of the time seem to us like a superior and solemn intrigue. Fundamentally, this was the nature of the subtle art of diplomacy. States were governed only by self-interest, but there were means of foiling or of falsifying the calculations of self-interest. The reason of state reigned; but passions governed and men were guided by them. Passions were the life-breath of statecraft, with the result that the latter was frequently lowered to the point of disgrace. The old Europe had no scruples and no pride in false delicacy. Yet the eighteenth century could show nothing more scandalous than the spectacle provided in the seventeenth by the court of Louis XIV, which Saint Simon described as "This trembling of the most powerful ministers and everyone of importance"—even the king of England, the queen and the ambassadors—before "the wretched widow of the famous cripple Scarron," the governess of the adulterine bastards of the king. Under Louis XV, the Empress Maria Theresa did not hesitate to seek out Madame de Pompadour. According to an official document, "she became the repository of the confidences which this ruler meant for the king." The empress opened her heart to the mistress of Louis XV in order to obtain the alliance of France. Several years later, when it was a question of obtaining recognition of the partition of Poland, carried out despite the alliance and against the wishes of Louis XV, she went farther. The deed was shady, so it was necessary to humiliate herself most profoundly. Maria Theresa's daughter of seventeen, Marie Antoinette, had just married the French dauphin. She charged her to cajole the royal mistress, Madame du Barry. She wrote to her ambassador: "I do not require sordidness and even less, intimacies, but rather the attentions due in consideration of her grandfather and her lord, in consideration of the good which may redound to us and to the two courts; perhaps the alliance depends on this. I await the results of your efforts and those of my daughter, knowing that you will employ every effort and she all her charms, in freeing herself from the prejudices which might be suggested to her against this course. No prejudices are as important as the good which she can do."

When the most respectable, most pious, and personally the most virtuous of sovereigns was reduced to such a surrender of principles, it is understandable that the complete skeptics who conducted affairs of state elsewhere moved with a singular ease on ground so well suited to their operations. If there were mistresses at Versailles, there were favorites at Petersburg who were won over by similar base means. Everywhere else the same game was played, sometimes carried to extremes, at least in intention, and well beyond the limits of gallantry. In 1723, an agent wrote to someone who desired the death of the king of Poland: "This event may not be so far off. Nothing is needed but a new mistress, spiritual and touching, to make it imminent for the king of Poland." One of the favorite artifices of diplomacy was to give a mistress to the king, a lover to the queen, to the empress, even to the princess royal, wife of the heir presumptive to the throne. The final audience and the secret instructions of such persons, who played a most important role and appeared for a long time on the great stage of the world, might be summed up in the celebrated couplet:

> And what, O king, do you command of me?
> To please this woman, and her lover be.

Corruption was the instrument in all these intrigues. Venality extended almost everywhere. With a proper pride, the Marquis d'Argenson reported a splendid exception to the general degradation. "Corruption has not slipped into the offices of foreign affairs in the slightest degree. This must be admitted as a phenomenon which is somewhat of a miracle and which does honor to the French nation in view of the low salaries paid to its clerks and the slight hope of advancement." D'Argenson claimed that the procedure "of agreeing to nothing without money in the hand" came from England. As a matter of fact, it was generally followed there, but it was also followed on the continent. The oldest treatises on the art of negotiation show this. La Bruyère placed among the qualities of the diplomat the art of knowing how to offer a bribe appropriately while also seeming ready to receive one. "He knows how to interest those with whom he treats, . . . neither does he wish to be thought unapproachable in the matter and permits a certain sensibility for his personal fortune to become apparent. In this way he attracts proposals which reveal to him the most secret views of the other side, their deepest designs, their final resource—and he profits by it."

In the eighteenth century, the majority of men did not stop with coquetting for bribes but profited from the system of corruption as much as possible. It was followed quite bluntly. In 1716 the Abbé Dubois negotiated with Lord Stanhope for the establishment of friendly relations between France and England. "I risked the suggestion," he wrote to the regent, "and I was overjoyed to see that he would let me mention everything, even the sum involved, which I fixed all at once at 600,000 livres, and which he heard graciously, without becoming angry." When the French revolution began, Baron Thugut, who had been the Austrian minister at Constantinople and who was to be called on to direct Austrian policy in this great crisis, had been receiving since 1768 a pension from the king of France. Aside from this steady business, there were the great markets of corruption which opened periodically—the diets of Sweden and of Poland. Those of Sweden in 1763 and 1766 cost France 1,400,000 and 1,800-

)oo livres respectively. In 1773 the Russian minister at Paris, ?anine, proposed to his colleagues at Vienna and Berlin to raise 'unds for bribery and to establish an account for their common operations.

The pre-eminent market, however, was the electoral diet of :he Holy Roman Empire. Everyone there was ready either to give or to receive. In 1741, when there was a proposal to raise a Bavarian to the imperial throne, Belle Isle opened the bidding. Nevertheless, as a prudent man, he would not pay until after the vote. This precaution was necessary, for the elector of Cologne, who had received 100,000 florins from Austria, had obtained permission from his confessor to go back on his word without returning the money. This procedure was even applied to the conclaves of cardinals in Rome. "The King," wrote a minister of Louis XIV, "should not omit any of the available means, and should employ adroitness and insinuations and even money, the most direct and certain means which has long been customary at the court of Rome, to insure the election of a wiser and less partial pope than the last." The section of secret funds and pensions occupied a pre-eminent place in the budgets of European chancelleries.

As if the cabals of official diplomacy were not enough and as if there were still work repugnant to it in these maneuvers of intrigue, corruption and fraud, it was parelleled by a secret diplomacy. This was entangled in its meshes and confused with it, and makes the history of negotiations in the eighteenth century an unsolvable labyrinth. There have always been secret agents to conduct delicate affairs or to open hazardous negotiations, but never have there been so many as in the eighteenth century. It seemed as if the sovereigns, satiated with absolute power, had acquired a sort of taste for romance, conspiracy and adventure. Their skepticism was so deep rooted, their distrust was so profound, and their abuse of stratagems had been carried to such a point that they had come to doubt everyone, and particularly their own confidants. To reassure them, unknown men were required who accosted them mysteriously with passwords and signs of recognition. A sort of diplomatic freemasonry was established, with its initiators and its adepts. What formerly had been an expedient became an institution. Louis XV carried this passion to the point of a mania, but in reality he did nothing but develop what had been done by others.

Europe was inundated with secret agents. The role they played seemed so flattering that it was generally sought. Financiers, who had correspondents everywhere, and men of letters, to whom all doors were opened, took pride in such employment, and found a new relish for their self-esteem in playing the part of negotiators and statesmen, if only in the antechambers of the great. In this role, Voltaire was pitiful, Diderot insignificant. F. M. Grimm, the German friend and correspondent of the Encyclopedists, had some understanding of the craft which he used to render service to his masters, and was even admitted among the regular practitioners. All ambitious men sought to climb by this back stairway. By this means Dumouriez launched his career. The registers of secret diplomacy are strewn with illustrious names, but none are more famous than those of the two men to whom the imminent death of Frederick the Great in 1786 provided the occasion for their introduction among the confidential agents in the background of diplomacy, from which they were soon to emerge to play the leading roles in the great revolutionary tragedy of the century. On the recommendation of Talleyrand, Mirabeau was sent as an observer to Berlin. It was like an improvised rehearsal in which they practiced each other's roles, Mirabeau taking the part of the ambassador and the future negotiator of the treaties of Vienna that of the minister without portfolio.

Adventurers abounded backstage and in the passages and wings of the diplomatic theatre. They encumbered the inns of the great cities, worming their way along the corridors, listening at all the keyholes, trafficking in secrets, selling news, veritable political panders ready to sell everything for which there was a demand and to buy everything which was for sale. Though the adventurer was "welcomed in one town, imprisoned in another," like Figaro, the hero and faithful image of Beaumarchais, he was more often welcomed than turned away. He was like a dealer in contraband goods, an exchange agent of an illegal bourse, or a travelling salesman for a clandestine trade. A cynic like Casanova and a charlatan like Cagliostro even penetrated the courts, and the Chevalier d'Éon, an equivocal adventurer and a kind of androgynous Figaro, made a place for himself in diplomacy. The Marquis de Poterat, an agitator and conspirator recently hunted by the police and the bailiff's men, a mixture of swindler, spy and literary blackmailer, a man irregular in every career, presented himself at Vienna with full powers from the French Directory—and was both received and heard. The Count d'Antraigues, who was no better, "the flower of scoundrels" as one of his employers called him, became "the soul" of the emigrant nobles from France, at whose head for a short time was another knight of the same stamp—Roques de Montgaillard.

The revolution in no way produced the bands of intriguers to be seen prowling on all the roads of Europe. They had grown in the depths like seaweed and the storm had only to tear them loose and toss them on the shore amid the wreckage and the foam. The time was propitious when they set to work, for the edifice of international society was overthrown and could be entered only from below. These adventurers were suited for this work. The custom of using men of this type already was established before 1789 and the greater number of them were known, though unfavorably. They were employed, and from this situation came the disproportionate significance which they acquired not only in the revolutionary party but in that of the emigrant nobles and even in the long-established courts.

Information was secured by surprising, corrupting or debauching agents, though such methods were rather dangerous and expensive. The simplest and least costly method of discovering the secrets of diplomats was to intercept their letters. According to Bielfeld's *Political Institutions*, "this breach of faith, seemingly authorized by common usage, is so well known and so incidental that practically everyone avoids the consequences by using an indecipherable code." But the key might be purchased, and there was no message, at least at that time, which did not in the end reveal its secret. The *black cabinet* was an institution of state, and the *intercepts*, as they were called, were a constant source of information. Certain agents became masters of the art of unsealing, deciphering and resealing letters. Those in Paris were considered especially adroit, but those in Vienna yielded nothing to them. They possessed not only the cipher of the French embassy but even that for the secret correspondence of Louis XV. By this crooked channel d'Aiguillon, the French minister of foreign affairs, learned the *secret of the king* [his plan to replace the Prussian alliance by one with Austria], which for a long time had not been a secret to the court of Vienna. The cardinal de Rohan, then ambassador at Vienna, had bribed one of the agents of the *black cabinet* and along with other precious documents revealed to him, found the letters which the Count de Broglie had sent to one of the embassy secretaries, unknown to the ambassador and the minister of foreign affairs.

The only way to avoid interceptions was to confide dispatches to reliable, brave and diligent couriers, and even this expedient was precarious enough. "Do not fail to code your dispatches carefully, even those you confide to Spanish couriers," wrote the Count de Montmorin to a French agent in Italy in 1788. "Not to mention other accidents, the Spanish couriers may be kidnapped, as has happened before." There were classic examples of this. In the month of June, 1685, Louvois, notified that a courier of the Emperor coming from Spain was to pass through Alsace, wrote to M. de Montclair, the commander at Strasbourg: "In the present situation, His Majesty considers it important to have this courier robbed and to secure his dispatches. Accordingly he orders you to place three or four reliable men in some village along the post road between Saverne and Strasbourg who are to rob this courier and take his dispatches, which are to be searched for with the greatest care, both on his person and in his saddle, under pretext of searching for money." If the courier defended himself he might lose his life. It might even be taken the better to create belief in an ambuscade by professional bandits. The wise

Bielfeld said, "Only strong men of recognized fidelity should be chosen for this rough career."

The couriers were unimportant people, and disappeared without leaving traces. Everyone knew that the roads were infested with brigands, and every government bore witness that their police were insufficient to repress them. To stop and rob the ambassadors themselves was more audacious and more difficult, but it was done nevertheless, in spite of the well known safeguards of international law. The precedents were notorious if not justifiable. The seizure of Maret and Sémonville, in Switzerland in 1793, was but a repetition of an attempt made in the same place under similar circumstances in the sixteenth century. French envoys crossing Milanese territory to go to the court of the Sultan Solyman the Magnificent were then assassinated by order of the imperial governor, who wished to secure their papers. The outrage at Rastadt, in 1799, when two of the French envoys to the congress were killed, also had its precedents, not so old it is true, but of the same high origin. During the Congress of Cologne in 1674, Louvois wrote to the Count d'Estrades: "It seems likely that M. de Lisola (the plenipotentiary of the Emperor) will leave Liège shortly to return to Cologne. It would be a great advantage to seize him, or even not greatly inconvenient to kill him in case he or those with him should defend themselves, because he is a most impertinent man whose every effort, and he does not lack industry, is directed against the interests of France with a terrible determination. You can hardly believe how much you will advance your interests before His Majesty by causing the execution of this project during his return." Lisola managed to escape from danger, but this method of negotiation was so customary that a month later the soldiers of the Emperor seized the prince of Furstenberg, the plenipotentiary of the elector of Cologne and a supporter of Louis XIV. They took him to Vienna, where he remained a prisoner until the peace was made.

The eighteenth century did but continue the tradition of violence and develop customary abuses. Frederick the Great carried the procedure of securing information by *intercepts* to its final development. In 1756, suspecting that a plot was being hatched against him and that the proof was to be found in Dresden, he occupied the city without a declaration of war and laid hands upon the archives of state. The lesson was not forgotten, and more than one application of it can be found in the history of Europe after the French revolution. The abduction of the Duke of Enghien from neutral territory, his summary sentence, and his secret execution in 1804 were in reality an ambush followed by assassination. The invasion of Rome by Napoleon in 1808, the arrest of the Pope and the seizure of the Vatican archives were but the final terms in a series begun under the old regime.

XII

PEACE, thus practiced, was precarious and perfidious, but war was atrocious. Nevertheless, though it seemed excessive and barbarous, war was better than peace in that it was straightforward and at least conformed to its purpose, which was the reign of force. It preserved a nobility derived from chivalry. Though the law which it made prevail—the law of the strongest—was crude and inferior, the means employed went far to redeem it. War demanded the highest virtues of which man felt himself capable. Honor reigned supreme. Among all who carried a sword a sort of fraternity of arms was established, which made them esteem each other even while they fought each other most fiercely. War was the aspect in which the old European society, and French society in particular, appeared in its finest form. Finally, arms provided the most noble of all careers, and one which followed the same rules in all the countries of Europe.

Wars were violent, but they were never racial conflicts, nor were they imbued with the bitterness of struggles between nations. Numbers of officers passed from the service of one state to that of another without incurring the slightest blame, much less suspicion of treason. The result was a high courtesy among the upper ranks before and after the combat which tempered to a certain degree the ferocity of war. The improvement, nevertheless, was slight. War stripped man of the superficial polish of civilization with which he was adorned. It laid him bare, revealing all his faults, releasing all his vices, unbridling all his passions. A most profound culture, the latent result of an old civilization, is necessary to preserve self-control in war. The men of the eighteenth century were still brutal and passionate beneath the surface of a refined elegance. Most of them discoursed elegantly on "humanity," but very few were humane. "Sensibility" was purely a matter of fashion. In culture as in costume, men powdered themselves and bedecked themselves in fine clothing, but fundamentally they kept all the crude ways of the preceding century. If it had been otherwise, neither the heroism nor the violence of the revolutionary wars could be explained. This violence was not the characteristic only of the improvised armies which the French republic threw into battle. It was found to the same degree in the army of the emigrant nobles, composed of aristocrats, and in the regular armies of the coalition of monarchs opposing the republic. It must not be forgotten that the wars of the revolution opened with the manifesto of the Duke of Brunswick which threatened the complete destruction of Paris. This manifesto was nothing more than the law of war under the old regime.

The history of the wars of the eighteenth century is like a sinister commentary on the etchings of Callot and Romain de Hooge. The soldiers appear to us brutal, the armies confused and without discipline. Implacability was the custom. War was expected to pay its way. Requisitions extended to the point of confiscation. All treasuries were emptied, even those of churches. The invader demanded the maximum ransoms the invaded could pay, not only as a means of supporting the army but as a means of filling the treasury and providing for future wars. The *extraordinary income from wars* was one of the surest resources of contemporary financiers. Add pillage, rape and fire, and the picture is complete. The burden of war fell upon the occupied country and crushed it. Inhabitants considered dangerous or simply suspect were proscribed. The others took fright and emigrated to escape the peril which menaced not only their goods but their persons, the honor of their wives and of their daughters. Then a tax was placed on absentees and, next, the houses of those who did not pay were demolished. Fire was the classic means of stimulating payments. "Attacks of fever," wrote the Duke of Luxembourg in 1672, "have never been as regular as our custom of burning out every other day those who were stupid enough to oblige us to do so." The Elector of the Palatinate protested, not against the thing but against its abuse. "It seems to me," he wrote to Turenne, "that, at most, only those localities where contributions are refused should be put to flame." Houses were burned and the inhabitants hanged in villages where troops were fired upon. A manifesto of July 25, 1792 stated: "The inhabitants of cities, towns and villages who dare to defend themselves against the troops of Their Imperial and Royal Majesties and fire upon them either in the open country or from windows, doors or openings in their houses shall be punished on the spot with the severity of martial law, and their houses shall be demolished or burned."

Louvois was the implacable executor of these bloody deeds, but he invented nothing; he only regularized, so to speak, the established usages and applied methodically the procedures which his contemporaries employed erratically. He held that this system of terror forced people into submission more rapidly. "It is absolutely necessary," he wrote with regard to the Palatinate, "to bring these people to reason, either by having them hanged or by burning their villages." The Germans put up a stubborn resistance; they rivaled the French in brutality; the cruelty of reprisals inflamed the passions. "We must outbid the Germans in inhumanity if they will not make war decently," cried Louvois. The Germans treated the French as "cannibals"; the French judged them to have but "the features and appearance of men." Louis XIV had fifty houses fired for one burned on his side; the Germans shot two French prisoners for each of their houses burned. If a fortified town resisted more than was usual, the garrison was threatened with being sent to the galleys. If emigrants or rebellious subjects were found in it, they were imprisoned. Then, if few in number, they were hanged; otherwise they were decimated and the survivors went to row in the galleys of the king. "I cannot refrain from telling you," wrote the Prince of Condé to Louvois in 1673, "that I find the spirits of these people quite different from the preceding year. They are all in despair. . . ." After 1793, this was to be the lugubrious and monotonous refrain of all the generals who were not mercenary brutes, and of all the commissioners who were not fanatics. The same complaints are found in the correspondence of foreign soldiers and diplomats. Foreign armies applied the martial law of Louvois to France, and the revolutionaries then applied it to foreign lands.

This was the way in which men of the eighteenth century understood war and waged it. D'Argenson received many complaints about it while minister of state, and was moved by them. He was told that "war and pity do not go together." It was true. The wars of the time were notorious for the indiscipline of armies, the exactions of victors, and the scandalous fortunes acquired by various leaders. Armies dragged along a parasitical mob hanging on their flanks and living off their spoil, ambulant suburbs where officers and soldiers went to sell and spend their booty. These devastating caravans moved cumbrously across the land, leaving ruin and disease behind them. They milled about in confusion and disbanded after a victory; they collapsed in disaster. After the passage of Frederick the Great's armies through Moravia in 1741, a contemporary wrote, "War waged in this fashion has not been seen since the Goths." In 1744, the Austrians pushed up to the frontier of Lorraine and summoned the inhabitants to submit. Those who resisted were hanged, "after being forced to cut off their own noses and ears."

The Seven Years War exceeded in atrocity all the preceding wars. In 1757 the Count of Saint Germain wrote: "The land for thirty leagues around is pillaged and ruined as if fire had passed over it." "We are surrounded by hanged corpses," reports another witness, "and women and children are still being massacred when they oppose the pillage of their own homes." Frederick incorporated prisoners in his army, and this was even a mercy for, on other occasions as at Crefeld, all who were beyond resistance were massacred. The animosity between Russians and Prussians was fearful. In 1757 the Russians occupied Memel, forced the garrison into their service and deported the citizens. "Nothing like it has been seen since the invasion of the Huns. Inhabitants were hanged after their noses and ears were cut off, their limbs were torn away, their entrails and hearts opened." The Prussians took their revenge the following year at Custrin.

"The Russians," recounted Frederick, "lost two thousand prisoners, and at least fifteen thousand men were left on the field because the soldiers gave them no quarter." In 1788 the Russian Prince Potemkin besieged the Turkish town of Ochakov for six months. He was a courtier and a man of the best taste. He took pride in literature and delicacy of feeling. "The cruelties of the Spanish in the new world and the English in the Indies," wrote a Russian, "are nothing in comparison with our military philosopher, who busied himself translating the *Heloise* of Rousseau while putting to death all who possessed goods capable of tempting his cupidity." On December 16 the assault was made. Of the twenty thousand Turks who defended the place, ten thousand were killed. The town was put to sack, the pillage lasted three days, and more than six thousand inhabitants were massacred. "The fury of the Russian soldiers was such," recounts Segur, "that, two days after the assault, when they found Turkish children hidden in certain refuges or cellars, they seized them, threw them into the air and caught them on the points of their bayonets, crying: 'At least these will never harm Christians!'"

Hostages were taken not only to ensure security on the march but also to protect detachments left in the rear. When he abandoned Prague in 1742, Belle Isle took with him sixteen notables chosen four from the nobility, four from the clergy, four from the magistrates and four from the citizens. They were to answer with their lives for the garrison which remained behind. In addition, places themselves were seized and whole countries occupied for the same reason. In 1757 the Duke of Choiseul wrote from Vienna: "I have engaged the Count of Kaunitz to state forcefully to the Hanoverian minister that the electorate of Hanover will answer for the damage if the 15,000 English troops which are expected to land in France make the least exaction contrary to the rules followed among civilized nations. Each French village fired by the English will result without remission in the burning of a Hanoverian town." Bernis, who was then the minister of foreign affairs, approved the measure entirely: "It would be too low an opinion of us to suppose that we are capable of sparing an enemy at bay. . . . The estates of the king of England [in Hanover] should be regarded as a sort of hostage in our hands."

To understand the ultimate development of the custom, and particularly that followed by the states forming the coalition against revolutionary France, one must consider what was done in countries occupied with the intention of annexation rather than in enemy lands invaded as a war measure. The Polish provinces which were to be partitioned in 1772 and which the powers seized as pledges to force the consent of the diet in Warsaw are an example. The Russian troops, "more highway robbers than soldiers" in the words of Rostopchine, rivaled and soon surpassed in violence the Poles whom they fought. On both sides men killed, pillaged, burned, raped and levied ransom in the name of religion. They converted each other with gunshot and whip lashes. A witness called the Russian commander Saldern "a madman to whom a saber had been given." Frederick of Prussia exploited for military purposes the territories he usurped. He collected stores of provisions, levied contributions, recruited his army, and requisitioned troops of female Poles to people Pomerania where, it seems, there was a lack of women. "Such harshness has driven the people to despair," wrote the Saxon resident.

The more cultivated Austrians prided themselves on legality. They delimited frontiers, examined titles to lands, established claims on them, and, this done, applied to the "reincorporated" populations the harsh government of the hereditary states of the Hapsburgs. Fundamentally, beneath these signs of moderation and forms of legal procedure, their rule was no lighter than that of the Russians and Prussians. "In the name of the beneficent Maria Theresa," reports one historian, "two men, Pergen, charged with administration, and Hadik, in command of the troops, took what were called revolutionary measures against these unhappy regions and applied there a law which went beyond that of our revolution." Emigration was imputed a crime and the inhabitants were forbidden to leave the territory. Those who remained were ransomed to the bone; those who sought to save themselves by flight from the odious occupation were punished by confiscation.

For example, Branicki, whom the king of Poland had sent on a mission to Versailles, was held to be an emigrant and his goods were confiscated. Polish judges were ordered to swear allegiance to Austria and condemn their compatriots upon every Austrian whim. The majority were afraid, and obeyed. In spite of all this, the court of Vienna supposed that these two proconsuls were too restrained and showed too much consideration. "Count Pergen is reproached here," wrote Joseph II, "for not being active enough, and the truth is that he has done nothing so far." Hadik was hardly better. "He is too old for this task, too slow, and hindered too much by his Hungarian prejudices, which are quite out of place there."

Such were the customs of war at the close of the old regime. The French terrorists of 1793 found them simple and accommodated themselves easily. At the same time they added to them a new and particularly insupportable depravity, aside from the ferocity of their fanaticism—humanitarian hypocrisy. It required unusual strength of character to resist the general trend, whether pushed by the tyranny of orders on one side or drawn by the contagion of general reprisals on the other. That it was done is the greatest glory of the heroes of the French national wars. Philosophical veterans like Dugommier and enthusiastic young warriors like Marceau or Desaix were able to enhance the military virtues of the old armies with the warm impulses of their own generous spirits.

XIII

To CONCLUDE, European custom on the eve of the French revolution is summed up in two events: the war of the Austrian succession and the partition of Poland. The first shows the low value placed on state engagements; the second the lack of respect for established sovereignties. These iniquitous deeds were the testament of the old Europe. Having signed it, she could only die, bequeathing the pernicious tradition of the abuses from which she perished to those who pretended to reform and knew only how to imitate her, to their own confusion and the public sorrow. These two abuses resulted from established European custom, but custom had never before been interpreted with such logical cynicism and pushed to such scandalous extremities in its application. Both events illustrate its ultimate development as well as its negation of law.

The old regime had reached the equivocal boundaries beyond which an unnatural law degenerates into an abuse. The example of past centuries, their own particular precedents, everything had disposed the states of Europe to such actions and drew them imperceptibly to such excesses of the sovereignty which was their principle of existence. They did not perceive that the excesses of state-selfishness destroyed the state itself. Their law was but prescription; it rested upon the fact of possession, which is because it is, and is sustained but by its own weight. *Mole sua stat.* With violence the rulers of the old regime tore the veil which hid the sanctuary of the state and kept from the mob the mystery of sovereignty. They showed the nations that two things surpassed the law of sovereigns and the law of states—the strength of states and the convenience of sovereigns. They opened the way to a revolution which needed but to turn against the established rulers their own conduct and follow their examples in order to upset their thrones and overthrow their empires. Thus by applying rigorously established custom, the sovereigns who represented most completely the old regime prepared its fall. Without knowing it, they justified this profound thought of Pascal: "Custom is the whole of equity and the sole reason for its acceptance; it is the mystical foundation of authority. He who brings equity back to its principle, destroys authority."

The reason of state as principle and so ultimate object, intrigue as the means, force as the sanction—these were all that remained of public law. "Force is the supreme law," said an Austrian diplomat, "and man is such that he must seek more when he already has enough." It was imposible to reflect on the situation without being frightened by it, and this impression of fright is given by all contemporaries who were a little above the scene, who observed and reflected. No one was more penetrated with it, nor described it in more striking terms, than Mallet du Pan, who was to be the ever clairvoyant and ever unheeded counsellor of the old Europe in the crisis which he foresaw. He wrote in 1792: "Perhaps in no other part of the world are there causes more pregnant with success for the authors of a social upheaval. Divided into a multitude of diverse governments, Europe offers few bases for a common resistance. The first great continental nation which changes the aspect of its society need fear but disunited members of the European body. As a result of the character which the polity of Europe has assumed since the last century and the nature of the conventions upon which it is founded, it has become difficult to stir up the thirty sovereigns of Europe in a common cause. They are all afraid of each other, and in the course of a hundred years their ministers have taught them to establish their particular safety on indifference to dangers threatening all other states which they suspect might be able to harm them in the future."

At the same time that the European republic dissolved into anarchy and the frail and artificial ties joining the governments seemed broken everywhere, similar principles of ruin and dissolution threatened the established order from within the states. Everything was decomposing and disintegrating at once. The same crisis disrupted the relations between states and disturbed at home the relations between government and citizens. In both cases, the crisis was produced by the same excesses and developed by the same causes. In foreign policy as in the internal affairs of states, the old regime perished from the abuse of its own principles. The same revolution threatened governments from all sides. Already powerless to league themselves against revolution if they divined its peril, they were even more powerless to discern it. The explanation of the way revolution could develop with impunity in Europe and triumph over the leagues formed to repress it lay hidden to them, and is revealed to us only by the study of European politics.

INDEX

ϽARPER ϟ ϾORϽHBOOϏS

IUMANITIES AND SOCIAL SCIENCES

merican Studies: General

NRY STEELE COMMAGER, Ed.: The Struggle for Racial
Equality   TB/1300
WARD S. CORWIN: American Constitutional History. △
Essays edited by Alpheus T. Mason and Gerald Gar-
vey   TB/1136
RL N. DEGLER, Ed.: Pivotal Interpretations of American
History   TB/1240; TB/1241
S. EISENSTADT, Ed.: The Craft of American History:
Recent Essays in American Historical Writing
Vol. I TB/1255; Vol. II TB/1256
ARLOTTE P. GILMAN: Women and Economics ‡ TB/3073
CAR HANDLIN, Ed.: This Was America: As Recorded
by European Travelers in the Eighteenth, Nineteenth
and Twentieth Centuries. Illus.   TB/1119
ARCUS LEE HANSEN: The Atlantic Migration: 1607-1860.
Edited by Arthur M. Schlesinger   TB/1052
ARCUS LEE HANSEN: The Immigrant in American His-
tory   TB/1120
HN HIGHAM, Ed.: The Reconstruction of American
History △   TB/1068
OBERT H. JACKSON: The Supreme Court in the American
System of Government   TB/1106
HN F. KENNEDY: A Nation of Immigrants. △ Illus.
                                                           TB/1118
ONARD W. LEVY, Ed.: American Constitutional Law
                                                           TB/1285
ONARD W. LEVY, Ed.: Judicial Review and the Supreme
Court   TB/1296
ONARD W. LEVY: The Law of the Commonwealth and
Chief Justice Shaw   TB/1309
ALPH BARTON PERRY: Puritanism and Democracy
                                                           TB/1138
RNOLD ROSE: The Negro in America: The Condensed
Version of Gunnar Myrdal's An American Dilemma
                                                           TB/3048
AURICE R. STEIN: The Eclipse of Community: An In-
terpretation of American Studies   TB/1128
. LLOYD WARNER: Social Class in America: The Evalua-
tion of Status   TB/1013

merican Studies: Colonial

ERNARD BAILYN, Ed.: The Apologia of Robert Keayne:
Self-Portrait of a Puritan Merchant   TB/1201
ERNARD BAILYN: The New England Merchants in the
Seventeenth Century   TB/1149
HARLES GIBSON: Spain in America †   TB/3077
AWRENCE HENRY GIPSON: The Coming of the Revolu-
tion: 1763-1775. † Illus.   TB/3007

PERRY MILLER: Errand Into the Wilderness   TB/1139
PERRY MILLER & T. H. JOHNSON, Eds.: The Puritans: A
Sourcebook   Vol. I TB/1093; Vol. II TB/1094
EDMUND S. MORGAN, Ed.: The Diary of Michael Wiggles-
worth, 1653-1657: The Conscience of a Puritan
                                                           TB/1228
EDMUND S. MORGAN: The Puritan Family: Religion and
Domestic Relations in Seventeenth-Century New
England   TB/1227
RICHARD B. MORRIS: Government and Labor in Early
America   TB/1244
KENNETH B. MURDOCK: Literature and Theology in
Colonial New England   TB/99
JOHN P. ROCHE: Origins of American Political Thought:
Selected Readings   TB/1301
JOHN SMITH: Captain John Smith's America: Selections
from His Writings. Ed. with Intro. by John Lankford
                                                           TB/3078
LOUIS B. WRIGHT: The Cultural Life of the American
Colonies: 1607-1763. † Illus.   TB/3005

American Studies: From the Revolution to 1860

JOHN R. ALDEN: The American Revolution: 1775-1783. †
Illus.   TB/3011
RAY A. BILLINGTON: The Far Western Frontier: 1830-
1860. † Illus.   TB/3012
EDMUND BURKE: On the American Revolution. ‡ Edited
by Elliott Robert Barkan   TB/3068
WHITNEY R. CROSS: The Burned-Over District: The Social
and Intellectual History of Enthusiastic Religion in
Western New York, 1800-1850   TB/1242
GEORGE DANGERFIELD: The Awakening of American Na-
tionalism: 1815-1828. † Illus.   TB/3061
CLEMENT EATON: The Freedom-of-Thought Struggle in
the Old South. Revised and Enlarged. Illus.   TB/1150
CLEMENT EATON: The Growth of Southern Civilization:
1790-1860. † Illus.   TB/3040
LOUIS FILLER: The Crusade Against Slavery: 1830-1860. †
Illus.   TB/3029
WILLIAM W. FREEHLING, Ed.: The Nullification Era: A
Documentary Record ‡   TB/3079
FELIX GILBERT: The Beginnings of American Foreign
Policy: To the Farewell Address   TB/1200
FRANCIS GRIERSON: The Valley of Shadows: The Coming
of the Civil War in Lincoln's Midwest: A Con-
temporary Account   TB/1246
ALEXANDER HAMILTON: The Reports of Alexander Ham-
ilton. ‡ Edited by Jacob E. Cooke   TB/3060
JAMES MADISON: The Forging of American Federalism:
Selected Writings of James Madison. Edited by Saul
K. Padover   TB/1126
BERNARD MAYO: Myths and Men: Patrick Henry, George
Washington, Thomas Jefferson   TB/1108

The New American Nation Series, edited by Henry Steele Commager and Richard B. Morris.
American Perspectives series, edited by Bernard Wishy and William E. Leuchtenburg.
† The Rise of Modern Europe series, edited by William L. Langer.
** History of Europe series, edited by J. H. Plumb.
‡ Researches in the Social, Cultural and Behavioral Sciences, edited by Benjamin Nelson.
The Library of Religion and Culture, edited by Benjamin Nelson.
ℰ Harper Modern Science Series, edited by James R. Newman.
* Not for sale in Canada.
△ Not for sale in the U. K.

JOHN C. MILLER: Alexander Hamilton and the Growth of the New Nation TB/3057

RICHARD B. MORRIS, Ed.: The Era of the American Revolution TB/1180

FRANCIS S. PHILBRICK: The Rise of the West, 1754-1830. † Illus. TB/3067

TIMOTHY L. SMITH: Revivalism and Social Reform: American Protestantism on the Eve of the Civil War TB/1229

ALBION W. TOURGÉE: A Fool's Errand ‡ TB/3074

GLYNDON G. VAN DEUSEN: The Jacksonian Era: 1828-1848. † Illus. TB/3028

LOUIS B. WRIGHT: Culture on the Moving Frontier TB/1053

American Studies: The Civil War to 1900

W. R. BROCK: An American Crisis: Congress and Reconstruction, 1865-67 ° △ TB/1283

THOMAS C. COCHRAN & WILLIAM MILLER: The Age of Enterprise: A Social History of Industrial America TB/1054

W. A. DUNNING: Reconstruction, Political and Economic: 1865-1877 TB/1073

HAROLD U. FAULKNER: Politics, Reform and Expansion: 1890-1900. † Illus. TB/3020

HELEN HUNT JACKSON: A Century of Dishonor: The Early Crusade for Indian Reform. ‡ Edited by Andrew F. Rolle TB/3063

ALBERT D. KIRWAN: Revolt of the Rednecks: Mississippi Politics, 1876-1925 TB/1199

ROBERT GREEN MC CLOSKEY: American Conservatism in the Age of Enterprise: 1865-1910 TB/1137

ARTHUR MANN: Yankee Reformers in the Urban Age: Social Reform in Boston, 1880-1900 TB/1247

WHITELAW REID: After the War: A Tour of the Southern States, 1865-1866. ‡ Edited by C. Vann Woodward TB/3066

CHARLES H. SHINN: Mining Camps: A Study in American Frontier Government. ‡ Edited by Rodman W. Paul TB/3062

VERNON LANE WHARTON: The Negro in Mississippi: 1865-1890 TB/1178

American Studies: 1900 to the Present

RAY STANNARD BAKER: Following the Color Line: American Negro Citizenship in Progressive Era. ‡ Illus. Edited by Dewey W. Grantham, Jr. TB/3053

RANDOLPH S. BOURNE: War and the Intellectuals: Collected Essays, 1915-1919. ‡ Ed. by Carl Resek TB/3043

A. RUSSELL BUCHANAN: The United States and World War II. † Illus. Vol. I TB/3044; Vol. II TB/3045

THOMAS C. COCHRAN: The American Business System: A Historical Perspective, 1900-1955 TB/1080

FOSTER RHEA DULLES: America's Rise to World Power: 1898-1954. † Illus. TB/3021

JOHN D. HICKS: Republican Ascendancy: 1921-1933. † Illus. TB/3041

SIDNEY HOOK: Reason, Social Myths, and Democracy TB/1237

ROBERT HUNTER: Poverty: Social Conscience in the Progressive Era. ‡ Edited by Peter d'A. Jones TB/3065

WILLIAM L. LANGER & S. EVERETT GLEASON: The Challenge to Isolation: The World Crisis of 1937-1940 and American Foreign Policy Vol. I TB/3054; Vol. II TB/3055

WILLIAM E. LEUCHTENBURG: Franklin D. Roosevelt and the New Deal: 1932-1940. † Illus. TB/3025

ARTHUR S. LINK: Woodrow Wilson and the Progressive Era: 1910-1917. † Illus. TB/3023

GEORGE E. MOWRY: The Era of Theodore Roosevelt and the Birth of Modern America: 1900-1912. † TB/3022

RUSSEL B. NYE: Midwestern Progressive Politics TB/1202

WILLIAM PRESTON, JR.: Aliens and Dissenters TB/1287

WALTER RAUSCHENBUSCH: Christianity and the Social Crisis. ‡ Edited by Robert D. Cross TB/3059

JACOB RIIS: The Making of an American. ‡ Edited by Roy Lubove TB/307

PHILIP SELZNICK: TVA and the Grass Roots: A Study in the Sociology of Formal Organization TB/1123

IDA M. TARBELL: The History of the Standard Oil Company. Briefer Version. ‡ Edited by David M. Chalmers TB/307

GEORGE B. TINDALL, Ed.: A Populist Reader ‡ TB/306

Anthropology

JACQUES BARZUN: Race: A Study in Superstition. Revised Edition TB/117

JOSEPH B. CASAGRANDE, Ed.: In the Company of Man: Portraits of Anthropological Informants TB/304

W. E. LE GROS CLARK: The Antecedents of Man: Intro to Evolution of the Primates. ° △ Illus. TB/559

CORA DU BOIS: The People of Alor. New Preface by the author. Illus. Vol. I TB/1042; Vol. II TB/1043

RAYMOND FIRTH, Ed.: Man and Culture: An Evaluation of the Work of Bronislaw Malinowski ¶ ° △ TB/1133

DAVID LANDY: Tropical Childhood: Cultural Transmission and Learning in a Puerto Rican Village ¶ TB/1235

L. S. B. LEAKEY: Adam's Ancestors: The Evolution of Man and His Culture. △ Illus. TB/1019

EDWARD BURNETT TYLOR: The Origin of Culture. Part I of "Primitive Culture." § Intro. by Paul Radin TB/33

EDWARD BURNETT TYLOR: Religion in Primitive Culture. Part II of "Primitive Culture." § Intro. by Paul Radin TB/34

Art and Art History

WALTER LOWRIE: Art in the Early Church. Revised Edition. 452 illus. TB/124

EMILE MÂLE: The Gothic Image: Religious Art in France of the Thirteenth Century. § △ 190 illus. TB/44

MILLARD MEISS: Painting in Florence and Siena after the Black Death: The Arts, Religion and Society in the Mid-Fourteenth Century. 169 illus. TB/1148

ERICH NEUMANN: The Archetypal World of Henry Moore. ° △ 107 illus. TB/2020

DORA & ERWIN PANOFSKY: Pandora's Box: The Changing Aspects of a Mythical Symbol. Illus. TB/2021

ALEXANDRE PIANKOFF: The Shrines of Tut-Ankh-Amon. Edited by N. Rambova. 117 illus. TB/2011

JEAN SEZNEC: The Survival of the Pagan Gods △ TB/2004

OTTO VON SIMSON: The Gothic Cathedral △ TB/2018

HEINRICH ZIMMER: Myths and Symbols in Indian Art and Civilization. 70 illustrations TB/2005

Business, Economics & Economic History

REINHARD BENDIX: Work and Authority in Industry TB/3035

THOMAS C. COCHRAN: The American Business System: A Historical Perspective, 1900-1955 TB/1080

THOMAS C. COCHRAN & WILLIAM MILLER: The Age of Enterprise: A Social History of Industrial America TB/1054

ROBERT DAHL & CHARLES E. LINDBLOM: Politics, Economics, and Welfare TB/3037

PETER F. DRUCKER: The New Society: The Anatomy of Industrial Order △ TB/1082

EDITORS OF FORTUNE: America in the Sixties: The Economy and the Society TB/1015

ROBERT L. HEILBRONER: The Great Ascent: The Struggle for Economic Development in Our Time TB/3030

ROBERT L. HEILBRONER: The Limits of American Capitalism TB/1305

FRANK H. KNIGHT: The Economic Organization TB/1214

FRANK H. KNIGHT: Risk, Uncertainty and Profit TB/1215

ABBA P. LERNER: Everybody's Business TB/3051

ROBERT GREEN MC CLOSKEY: American Conservatism in the Age of Enterprise, 1865-1910 TB/1137

PAUL MANTOUX: The Industrial Revolution in the Eighteenth Century ° △ TB/1079

3

HAJO HOLBORN: Ulrich von Hutten and the German Reformation TB/1238

JOHAN HUIZINGA: Erasmus and the Age of Reformation.△ *Illus.* TB/19

JOEL HURSTFIELD, Ed.: The Reformation Crisis △ TB/1267

ULRICH VON HUTTEN et al.: On the Eve of the Reformation: "Letters of Obscure Men" TB/1124

PAUL O. KRISTELLER: Renaissance Thought: *The Classic, Scholastic, and Humanist Strains* TB/1048

PAUL O. KRISTELLER: Renaissance Thought II: *Papers on Humanism and the Arts* TB/1163

NICCOLÒ MACHIAVELLI: History of Florence and of the Affairs of Italy TB/1027

ALFRED VON MARTIN: Sociology of the Renaissance. *Introduction by Wallace K. Ferguson* △ TB/1099

GARRETT MATTINGLY et al.: Renaissance Profiles. △ *Edited by J. H. Plumb* TB/1162

MILLARD MEISS: Painting in Florence and Siena after the Black Death: *The Arts, Religion and Society in the Mid-Fourteenth Century.* △ *169 illus.* TB/1148

J. E. NEALE: The Age of Catherine de Medici ○ △ TB/1085

ERWIN PANOFSKY: Studies in Iconology: *Humanistic Themes in the Art of the Renaissance* △ TB/1077

J. H. PARRY: The Establishment of the European Hegemony: 1415-1715 △ TB/1045

J. H. PLUMB: The Italian Renaissance: *A Concise Survey of Its History and Culture* △ TB/1161

A. F. POLLARD: Henry VIII. ○ △ *Introduction by A. G. Dickens* TB/1249

A. F. POLLARD: Wolsey. ○ △ *Introduction by A. G. Dickens* TB/1248

CECIL ROTH: The Jews in the Renaissance. *Illus.* TB/834

A. L. ROWSE: The Expansion of Elizabethan England. ○ △ *Illus.* TB/1220

GORDON RUPP: Luther's Progress to the Diet of Worms ○ △ TB/120

G. M. TREVELYAN: England in the Age of Wycliffe, 1368-1520 ○ △ TB/1112

VESPASIANO: Renaissance Princes, Popes, and Prelates: *The Vespasiano Memoirs: Lives of Illustrious Men of the XVth Century* TB/1111

History: Modern European

FREDERICK B. ARTZ: Reaction and Revolution, 1815-1852. * *Illus.* TB/3034

MAX BELOFF: The Age of Absolutism, 1660-1815 △ TB/1062

ROBERT C. BINKLEY: Realism and Nationalism, 1852-1871. * *Illus.* TB/3038

ASA BRIGGS: The Making of Modern England, 1784-1867: *The Age of Improvement* ○ △ TB/1203

CRANE BRINTON: A Decade of Revolution, 1789-1799. * *Illus.* TB/3018

D. W. BROGAN: The Development of Modern France. ○ △
Volume I: *From the Fall of the Empire to the Dreyfus Affair* TB/1184
Volume II: *The Shadow of War, World War I, Between the Two Wars. New Introduction by the Author* TB/1185

J. BRONOWSKI & BRUCE MAZLISH: The Western Intellectual Tradition: *From Leonardo to Hegel* △ TB/3001

GEOFFREY BRUUN: Europe and the French Imperium, 1799-1814. * *Illus.* TB/3033

ALAN BULLOCK: Hitler, A Study in Tyranny ○ △ TB/1123

E. H. CARR: German-Soviet Relations between the Two World Wars, 1919-1939 TB/1278

E. H. CARR: International Relations between the Two World Wars, 1919-1939 ○ △ TB/1279

E. H. CARR: The Twenty Years' Crisis, 1919-1939 ○ △ TB/1122

GORDON A. CRAIG: From Bismarck to Adenauer: *Aspects of German Statecraft. Revised Edition* TB/1171

DENIS DIDEROT: The Encyclopedia: *Selections. Ed and trans. by Stephen Gendzier* TB/1299

WALTER L. DORN: Competition for Empire, 1740-1763. * *Illus.* TB/303

FRANKLIN L. FORD: Robe and Sword: *The Regrouping of the French Aristocracy after Louis XIV* TB/121

CARL J. FRIEDRICH: The Age of the Baroque, 1610-1660. * *Illus.* TB/300

RENÉ FUELOEP-MILLER: The Mind and Face of Bolshevism TB/1188

M. DOROTHY GEORGE: London Life in the Eighteenth Century △ TB/118

LEO GERSHOY: From Despotism to Revolution, 1763-1789. * *Illus.* TB/3017

C. C. GILLISPIE: Genesis and Geology: *The Decades before Darwin* § TB/5

ALBERT GOODWIN: The French Revolution △ TB/1064

ALBERT GUÉRARD: France in the Classical Age: *The Life and Death of an Ideal* △ TB/118

CARLTON J. H. HAYES: A Generation of Materialism, 1871-1900. * *Illus.* TB/3039

STANLEY HOFFMANN et al.: In Search of France TB/1219

A. R. HUMPHREYS: The Augustan World: *Society, Thought, and Letters in 18th Century England* ○ △ TB/1105

DAN N. JACOBS, Ed.: The New Communist Manifesto *& Related Documents. Third edition, Revised* TB/1078

LIONEL KOCHAN: The Struggle for Germany: *1914-45* TB/1304

HANS KOHN: The Mind of Germany △ TB/120

HANS KOHN, Ed.: The Mind of Modern Russia: *Historical and Political Thought of Russia's Great Age* TB/1065

WALTER LAQUEUR & GEORGE L. MOSSE, Eds.: International Fascism, 1920-1945 ○ △ TB/1276

WALTER LAQUEUR & GEORGE L. MOSSE, Eds.: The Left-Wing Intellectuals between the Wars, 1919-1939 ○ △ TB/1286

WALTER LAQUEUR & GEORGE L. MOSSE, Eds.: 1914: *The Coming of the First World War* ○ △ TB/1306

FRANK E. MANUEL: The Prophets of Paris: *Turgot, Condorcet, Saint-Simon, Fourier, and Comte* TB/1218

KINGSLEY MARTIN: French Liberal Thought in the Eighteenth Century TB/1114

L. B. NAMIER: Facing East △ TB/1280

L. B. NAMIER: Personalities and Powers: *Selected Essays* △ TB/1186

L. B. NAMIER: Vanished Supremacies: *Essays on European History, 1812-1918* ○ △ TB/1088

JOHN U. NEF: Western Civilization Since the Renaissance: *Peace, War, Industry, and the Arts* TB/1113

FRANZ NEUMANN: Behemoth: *The Structure and Practice of National Socialism, 1933-1944* TB/1289

FREDERICK L. NUSSBAUM: The Triumph of Science and Reason, 1660-1685. * *Illus.* TB/3009

DAVID OGG: Europe of the Ancien Régime, 1715-1783 ** ○ △ TB/1271

JOHN PLAMENATZ: German Marxism and Russian Communism. ○ △ *New Preface by the Author* TB/1189

RAYMOND W. POSTGATE, Ed.: Revolution from 1789 to 1906: *Selected Documents* TB/1063

PENFIELD ROBERTS: The Quest for Security, 1715-1740. * *Illus.* TB/3016

PRISCILLA ROBERTSON: Revolutions of 1848: *A Social History* TB/1025

GEORGE RUDÉ: Revolutionary Europe, 1783-1815 ** ○ △ TB/1272

LOUIS, DUC DE SAINT-SIMON: Versailles, The Court, and Louis XIV. △ *Introductory Note by Peter Gay* TB/1250

ALBERT SOREL: Europe Under the Old Regime. *Translated by Francis H. Herrick* TB/1121

N. N. SUKHANOV: The Russian Revolution, 1917: *Eyewitness Account.* △ *Edited by Joel Carmichael*
Vol. I TB/1066; Vol. II TB/1067

A. J. P. TAYLOR: From Napoleon to Lenin: *Historical Essays* ○ △ TB/1268

A. J. P. TAYLOR: The Habsburg Monarchy, 1809-1918 ○ △ TB/1187

4

Political Science & Government

Psychology

G. JUNG & C. KERÉNYI: Essays on a Science of Mythology: *The Myths of the Divine Child and the Divine Maiden* TB/2014

HN T. MC NEILL: A History of the Cure of Souls TB/126

ARL MENNINGER: Theory of Psychoanalytic Technique TB/1144

LICH NEUMANN: Amor and Psyche △ TB/2012

RICH NEUMANN: The Archetypal World of Henry Moore. *107 illus.* TB/2020

LICH NEUMANN: The Origins and History of Consciousness △ Vol. I *Illus.* TB/2007; Vol. II TB/2008

P. OBERNDORF: A History of Psychoanalysis in America TB/1147

ALPH BARTON PERRY: The Thought and Character of William James: *Briefer Version* TB/1156

AN PIAGET, BÄRBEL INHELDER, & ALINA SZEMINSKA: The Child's Conception of Geometry ∘ △ TB/1146

OHN H. SCHAAR: Escape from Authority: *The Perspectives of Erich Fromm* TB/1155

UZAFER SHERIF: The Psychology of Social Norms TB/3072

ociology

ACQUES BARZUN: Race: *A Study in Superstition. Revised Edition* TB/1172

ERNARD BERELSON, Ed.: The Behavioral Sciences Today TB/1127

BRAHAM CAHAN: The Rise of David Levinsky: *A documentary novel of social mobility in early twentieth century America. Intro. by John Higham* TB/1028

HOMAS C. COCHRAN: The Inner Revolution: *Essays on the Social Sciences in History* TB/1140

EWIS A. COSER, Ed.: Political Sociology TB/1293

ALLISON DAVIS & JOHN DOLLARD: Children of Bondage: *The Personality Development of Negro Youth in the Urban South* ¶ TB/3049

T. CLAIR DRAKE & HORACE R. CAYTON: Black Metropolis: *A Study of Negro Life in a Northern City. Revised and Enlarged. Intro. by Everett C. Hughes* Vol. I TB/1086; Vol. II TB/1087

ÉMILE DURKHEIM et al.: Essays on Sociology and Philosophy. *With Analysis of Durkheim's Life and Work.* ¶ *Edited by Kurt H. Wolff* TB/1151

EON FESTINGER, HENRY W. RIECKEN & STANLEY SCHACHTER: When Prophecy Fails: *A Social and Psychological Account of a Modern Group that Predicted the Destruction of the World* ¶ TB/1132

ALVIN W. GOULDNER: Wildcat Strike ¶ TB/1176

FRANCIS J. GRUND: Aristocracy in America: *Social Class in the Formative Years of the New Nation* △ TB/1001

KURT LEWIN: Field Theory in Social Science: *Selected Theoretical Papers* ¶ △ *Edited with a Foreword by Dorwin Cartwright* TB/1135

R. M. MAC IVER: Social Causation TB/1153

ROBERT K. MERTON, LEONARD BROOM, LEONARD S. COTTRELL, JR., Editors: Sociology Today: *Problems and Prospects* ¶ Vol. I TB/1173; Vol. II TB/1174

ROBERTO MICHELS: First Lectures in Political Sociology. *Edited by Alfred de Grazia* ¶ ∘ TB/1224

BARRINGTON MOORE, JR.: Political Power and Social Theory: *Seven Studies* ¶ TB/1221

BARRINGTON MOORE, JR.: Soviet Politics — The Dilemma of Power: *The Role of Ideas in Social Change* ¶ TB/1222

TALCOTT PARSONS & EDWARD A. SHILS, Editors: Toward a General Theory of Action TB/1083

JOHN H. ROHRER & MUNRO S. EDMONSON, Eds.: The Eighth Generation Grows Up ¶ TB/3050

KURT SAMUELSSON: Religion and Economic Action: *A Critique of Max Weber's* The Protestant Ethic and the Spirit of Capitalism. ¶ ∘ *Trans. by E. G. French. Ed. with Intro. by D. C. Coleman* TB/1131

PHILIP SELZNICK: TVA and the Grass Roots: *A Study in the Sociology of Formal Organization* TB/1230

GEORG SIMMEL et al.: Essays on Sociology, Philosophy, and Aesthetics. ¶ *Edited by Kurt H. Wolff* TB/1234

HERBERT SIMON: The Shape of Automation △ TB/1245

PITIRIM A. SOROKIN: Contemporary Sociological Theories: *Through the First Quarter of the 20th Century* TB/3046

MAURICE R. STEIN: The Eclipse of Community: *An Interpretation of American Studies* TB/1128

FERDINAND TÖNNIES: Community and Society: *Gemeinschaft und Gesellschaft. Translated and edited by Charles P. Loomis* TB/1116

W. LLOYD WARNER & Associates: Democracy in Jonesville: *A Study in Quality and Inequality* TB/1129

W. LLOYD WARNER: Social Class in America: *The Evaluation of Status* TB/1013

RELIGION

Ancient & Classical

J. H. BREASTED: Development of Religion and Thought in Ancient Egypt TB/57

HENRI FRANKFORT: Ancient Egyptian Religion TB/77

G. RACHEL LEVY: Religious Conceptions of the Stone Age and their Influence upon European Thought. △ *Illus. Introduction by Henri Frankfort* TB/106

MARTIN P. NILSSON: Greek Folk Religion TB/78

ALEXANDRE PIANKOFF: The Shrines of Tut-Ankh-Amon. △ *Edited by N. Rambova. 117 illus.* TB/2011

ERWIN ROHDE: Psyche Vol. I TB/140; Vol. II TB/141

H. J. ROSE: Religion in Greece and Rome △ TB/55

Biblical Thought & Literature

W. F. ALBRIGHT: The Biblical Period from Abraham to Ezra TB/102

C. K. BARRETT, Ed.: The New Testament Background: *Selected Documents* △ TB/86

C. H. DODD: The Authority of the Bible △ TB/43

M. S. ENSLIN: Christian Beginnings △ TB/5

M. S. ENSLIN: The Literature of the Christian Movement △ TB/6

JOHN GRAY: Archaeology and the Old Testament World. △ *Illus.* TB/127

JAMES MUILENBURG: The Way of Israel: *Biblical Faith and Ethics* △ TB/133

H. H. ROWLEY: The Growth of the Old Testament △ TB/107

G. A. SMITH: The Historical Geography of the Holy Land TB/138

D. WINTON THOMAS, Ed.: Documents from Old Testament Times △ TB/85

WALTHER ZIMMERLI: The Law and the Prophets: *A Study of the Meaning of the Old Testament* △ TB/144

The Judaic Tradition

LEO BAECK: Judaism and Christianity. *Trans. with Intro. by Walter Kaufmann* TB/823

SALO W. BARON: Modern Nationalism and Religion JP/18

MARTIN BUBER: Eclipse of God: *Studies in the Relation Between Religion and Philosophy* △ TB/12

MARTIN BUBER: For the Sake of Heaven TB/801

MARTIN BUBER: Hasidism and Modern Man △ TB/839

MARTIN BUBER: The Knowledge of Man: *Selected Essays.* △ *Edited with an Introduction by Maurice Friedman. Translated by Maurice Friedman and Ronald Gregor Smith* TB/135

MARTIN BUBER: Moses: *The Revelation and the Covenant* △ TB/827

MARTIN BUBER: The Origin and Meaning of Hasidism △ TB/835

MARTIN BUBER: Pointing the Way. △ *Introduction by Maurice S. Friedman* TB/103

MARTIN BUBER: The Prophetic Faith TB/73

MARTIN BUBER: Two Types of Faith: *the interpenetration of Judaism and Christianity* ∘ △ TB/75

ERNST LUDWIG EHRLICH: A Concise History of Israel: *From the Earliest Times to the Destruction of the Temple in A.D. 70* ∘ △ TB/128

NATURAL SCIENCES
AND MATHEMATICS

HAROLD F. BLUM: Time's Arrow and Evolution   TB/555
JOHN TYLER BONNER: The Ideas of Biology. Σ △ Illus.   TB/570
A. J. CAIN: Animal Species and their Evolution. △ Illus.   TB/519
WALTER B. CANNON: Bodily Changes in Pain, Hunger, Fear and Rage. Illus.   TB/562
W. E. LE GROS CLARK: The Antecedents of Man: Intro. to Evolution of the Primates. ○ △ Illus.   TB/559
W. H. DOWDESWELL: Animal Ecology. △ Illus.   TB/543
W. H. DOWDESWELL: The Mechanism of Evolution. △ Illus.   TB/527
R. W. GERARD: Unresting Cells. Illus.   TB/541
DAVID LACK: Darwin's Finches. △ Illus.   TB/544
ADOLF PORTMANN: Animals as Social Beings. ○ △ Illus.   TB/572
O. W. RICHARDS: The Social Insects. △ Illus.   TB/542
P. M. SHEPPARD: Natural Selection and Heredity. Illus.   TB/528
EDMUND W. SINNOTT: Cell and Psyche: The Biology of Purpose   TB/546
C. H. WADDINGTON: How Animals Develop. △ Illus.   TB/553
C. H. WADDINGTON: The Nature of Life: The Main Problems and Trends in Modern Biology △   TB/580

Chemistry

J. R. PARTINGTON: A Short History of Chemistry. △ Illus.   TB/522

Communication Theory

J. R. PIERCE: Symbols, Signals and Noise: The Nature and Process of Communication △   TB/574

Geography

R. E. COKER: This Great and Wide Sea: An Introduction to Oceanography and Marine Biology. Illus.   TB/551
F. K. HARE: The Restless Atmosphere △   TB/560

History of Science

MARIE BOAS: The Scientific Renaissance, 1450-1630 ○ △   TB/583
W. DAMPIER, Ed.: Readings in the Literature of Science. Illus.   TB/512
A. HUNTER DUPREE: Science in the Federal Government: A History of Policies and Activities to 1940 △   TB/573
ALEXANDRE KOYRÉ: From the Closed World to the Infinite Universe: Copernicus, Kepler, Galileo, Newton, etc. △   TB/31
A. G. VAN MELSEN: From Atomos to Atom: A History of the Concept Atom   TB/517
O. NEUGEBAUER: The Exact Sciences in Antiquity   TB/552
HANS THIRRING: Energy for Man: From Windmills to Nuclear Power △   TB/556
STEPHEN TOULMIN & JUNE GOODFIELD: The Architecture of Matter ○ △   TB/584
STEPHEN TOULMIN & JUNE GOODFIELD: The Discovery of Time ○ △   TB/585
LANCELOT LAW WHYTE: Essay on Atomism: From Democritus to 1960 △   TB/565

Mathematics

E. W. BETH: The Foundations of Mathematics: A Stu in the Philosophy of Science △   TB/5
H. DAVENPORT: The Higher Arithmetic: An Introducti to the Theory of Numbers △   TB/5
H. G. FORDER: Geometry: An Introduction △   TB/5
S. KÖRNER: The Philosophy of Mathematics: An Intr duction △   TB/5
D. E. LITTLEWOOD: Skeleton Key of Mathematics: Simple Account of Complex Algebraic Problems △   TB/5
GEORGE E. OWEN: Fundamentals of Scientific Math matics   TB/5
WILLARD VAN ORMAN QUINE: Mathematical Logic TB/5
O. G. SUTTON: Mathematics in Action. ○ △ Foreword James R. Newman. Illus.   TB/5
FREDERICK WAISMANN: Introduction to Mathematic Thinking. Foreword by Karl Menger   TB/5

Philosophy of Science

R. B. BRAITHWAITE: Scientific Explanation   TB/5
J. BRONOWSKI: Science and Human Values. △ Revised an Enlarged Edition   TB/5
ALBERT EINSTEIN et al.: Albert Einstein: Philosophe Scientist. Edited by Paul A. Schilpp   Vol. I TB/5   Vol. II TB/5
WERNER HEISENBERG: Physics and Philosophy: The Reve lution in Modern Science △   TB/54
JOHN MAYNARD KEYNES: A Treatise on Probability. ○ Introduction by N. R. Hanson   TB/55
KARL R. POPPER: Logic of Scientific Discovery △   TB/57
STEPHEN TOULMIN: Foresight and Understanding: A Enquiry into the Aims of Science. △ Foreword b Jacques Barzun   TB/56
STEPHEN TOULMIN: The Philosophy of Science: An In troduction △   TB/5
G. J. WHITROW: Natural Philosophy of Time ○ △   TB/56

Physics and Cosmology

JOHN E. ALLEN: Aerodynamics: A Space Age Survey △   TB/58
STEPHEN TOULMIN & JUNE GOODFIELD: The Fabric of th Heavens: The Development of Astronomy and Dy namics. △ Illus.   TB/57
DAVID BOHM: Causality and Chance in Modern Physics. Foreword by Louis de Broglie   TB/53
P. W. BRIDGMAN: The Nature of Thermodynamics   TB/53
P. W. BRIDGMAN: A Sophisticate's Primer of Relativity   TB/57
A. C. CROMBIE, Ed.: Turning Point in Physics   TB/53
C. V. DURRELL: Readable Relativity. △ Foreword by Free man J. Dyson   TB/53
ARTHUR EDDINGTON: Space, Time and Gravitation: A Outline of the General Relativity Theory   TB/51
GEORGE GAMOW: Biography of Physics Σ △   TB/56
MAX JAMMER: Concepts of Force: A Study in the Founda tion of Dynamics   TB/55
MAX JAMMER: Concepts of Mass in Classical and Moder Physics   TB/57
MAX JAMMER: Concepts of Space: The History o Theories of Space in Physics. Foreword by Alber Einstein   TB/53
G. J. WHITROW: The Structure and Evolution of the Uni verse: An Introduction to Cosmology. △ Illus.   TB/50

DATE DUE